MANCHESTER ON A PLATE

MANCHESTER ON A PLATE

PHOTOGRAPHS BY PAUL DODDS

BLACK & WHITE PUBLISHING

First published 2002
by Black & White Publishing Ltd, Edinburgh
ISBN 1 902927 30 3

British Library Cataloguing in Publication data:
a catalogue record for this book is available from The British Library.

Design concept by Navy Blue

Printed and bound in Spain by
Book Print, S.L., Barcelona

Contents

We have reproduced the recipes as supplied by the chefs,
according to their own individual cooking styles.
All recipes serve four, unless otherwise stated.

Foreword
by Steven Saunders

Call me biased, but as someone intimately involved in Manchester's culinary renaissance through my work at The Lowry, I can vouch for the diversity and quality of the food that this city has to offer.

The vibrancy of the restaurant scene here is renowned throughout Europe – and justifiably so. Leading exponents of cookery from all four corners of the globe can be found in Manchester, reflecting and enhancing the city's unique multi-cultural mix. People now expect the best – the highest of standards and the most creative of menus, and the city never fails to satisfy.

But can a book ever hope to capture such flavours? I am delighted to say it can. In the mouth-watering pages that follow you'll find Venetian tastes rubbing shoulders with Korean, and French techniques alongside Chinese and East Asian. What's more, I am particularly pleased that British cuisine – more particularly northern English cooking – plays its part with dishes like the duck and black pudding sausages from Ian Morgan at Rhodes and Co, and Dave Aspin's Manchester smoothie at Simply Heathcotes.

This book is a celebration of the best cooking that Manchester has to offer. I hope you enjoy recreating the sumptuous dishes it contains, and are tempted to go out and sample them by visiting the restaurants featured.

Dave Aspin
Simply Heathcotes

Dave Aspin
Simply Heathcotes

Heathcotes has been an important part of my life since it opened five years ago. I worked my way up through the ranks here, was Sous Chef for a year, became Head Chef in November 2000, and have to say that I really do enjoy every single day.

As you'll see from the dishes I've chosen, we specialise in good British food with a northern influence and a modern twist. Only the highest quality of ingredients are used in our recipes because we take time to source the best produce from carefully selected suppliers. But in a sense that is only half the story. It is just as important to us that the atmosphere of the restaurant allows our customers to feel relaxed and comfortable, and we go to extraordinary lengths to make sure that each meal is a memorable occasion every time. This means that all the members of the team must be highly skilled and passionate about their work. My ambition is to be as good as I can in my chosen profession and for my team to be the guardians of the Heathcotes reputation so that it retains its place as the leading restaurant for dining out in Manchester.

Goats cheese hash browns

with apple compote and grain mustard butter

for the hash browns
500g Maris Piper potatoes
1tsp chives, snipped
1tsp parsley, finely chopped
1 medium egg white, lightly
whisked
salt and freshly ground black
pepper
200g goats cheese, cut into 4
sunflower oil for frying

for the apple compote
25g unsalted butter
2 Bramley apples, peeled and
chopped
1 sprig of fresh rosemary
caster sugar to taste

for the mustard butter
1tsp white wine vinegar
2tsp dry white wine
2 shallots, peeled and very finely
chopped
1tsp double cream
100g hard unsalted butter, diced
salt and freshly ground white
pepper
1tbsp whole grain mustard

other ingredients
salad leaves to garnish

For the hash browns: bring the potatoes to the boil in seasoned water, cook them until just firm, drain and leave them to cool. Peel the potatoes and grate them into a bowl, stirring in the chives, parsley and egg white with a pinch of salt and pepper. Pat out a quarter of the mixture into a circle that is larger in diameter than the goats cheese and place the goats cheese in the middle. Fold the potato around the outside, repeating with the remaining potato and goats cheese. Heat the oil to 160°C and deep-fry the hash browns until golden brown on all sides. Remove and drain them on kitchen paper, keeping them warm until required.

For the apple compote: melt the butter in a pan and, when foaming, add the apples and rosemary. Cook them until the apple is soft, adding a little sugar if necessary, then pass the apples through a fine sieve and keep the mixture warm.

For the mustard butter: place the vinegar, wine and shallots in a small pan and reduce them to a syrup. Add the cream and mustard, reduce a little more, then whisk in the butter until blended. Season to taste, pass everything through a fine sieve and add the mustard.

To serve, place the apple compote in the centre of the dish with the hash brown on top. Drizzle the sauce around the edge and garnish with a few salad leaves on top.

Pot-roasted rib eye of pork

with black pudding, cider potatoes and caramelised chicory

4 slices black pudding, cooked

for the pork
4 x 200g rib eye of pork
3tbsp olive oil
1 small onion, peeled and finely chopped
2 carrots, peeled and finely chopped
1 stick celery, peeled and finely chopped
2 cloves of garlic, crushed
100ml red wine
salt and white pepper

for the caramelised chicory
2 chicory, cut in half
50g caster sugar

for the cider potatoes
2 baking potatoes, peeled and halved
75g unsalted butter
100ml dry cider
a pinch of salt

For the pork: preheat the oven to 170°C (gas mark 3). Warm the oil in an ovenproof dish, season the pork and seal it in the oil. When browned on both sides, add the chopped vegetables and garlic and continue to cook for 5 minutes. Pour in the wine, cover with a lid and place in the oven for 40 minutes or until cooked.

For the caramelised chicory: blanch the chicory in seasoned water until cooked, then refresh in iced water. Caramelise the sugar in a separate pan, and coat the chicory with it, keeping it warm until needed.

For the cider potatoes: cook all ingredients together in the oven or on the stove. When the potatoes are a golden colour on one side, turn them over and cook them on the other side until they are cooked through and glazed.

To serve, place the potato on the dish with the chicory resting beside it. Position the pork next to this, with the cooked black pudding on top, and pour the red wine sauce around. If desired, serve on a bed of shredded cabbage.

Seared tuna

with sweet and sour vegetables, and tomato
and tarragon dressing

4 x 120g tuna steaks
2tbsp olive oil
for the pickling liquor
250ml water
50ml white wine vinegar
1 fresh bay leaf
50g clear honey
1 sprig of fresh thyme, whole
2 cloves of garlic, roughly
chopped
2 shallots, chopped
**for the sweet and sour
vegetables**
1 carrot, finely sliced
1 courgette, finely sliced
1 stick celery, finely sliced
1 medium onion, finely sliced
**for the tomato and tarragon
dressing**
100ml virgin olive oil
15ml tarragon vinegar
(readymade)
50g shallots, finely chopped
60g Heinz ketchup
6g fresh tarragon, chopped
salt
for the garnish
rocket leaves

For the pickling liquor: bring the ingredients to the boil and leave to stand for 20 minutes.

For the sweet and sour vegetables: blanch the vegetables in seasoned water, refresh in iced water and drain, before adding the hot pickling liquor. Leave them to marinate.

To prepare the dish, mix the ingredients for the dressing together. Sear the tuna in a hot pan with a little oil for 1 ½ minutes on each side. Place the vegetables in the middle of the dish with the seared tuna on top and a cordon of tomato and tarragon dressing around the edge. Garnish with rocket leaves.

Manchester smoothie

chocolate cookies, Thwaites ice-cream and vanilla
and chocolate sauce

for the chocolate cookies

250g unsalted butter
80g dark chocolate
300g light brown sugar
40g dark brown sugar
1–2 whole eggs
seeds from 3 vanilla pods
300g plain flour
1tsp bicarbonate of soda
125g cocoa powder
60g chocolate chips

for the beer ice-cream

100g caster sugar
6 egg yolks
350ml whipping cream
150ml creamy beer

for the chocolate sauce

125ml water
80g caster sugar
seeds from 1 vanilla pod
25g couverture chocolate (dark,
high cocoa content)
8g cornflour
20g cocoa powder

For the chocolate cookies: preheat the oven to 180°C (gas mark 4).
Cream together the butter, dark chocolate and sugar, then beat in the
eggs and vanilla seeds. Sieve in the flour, bicarbonate of soda and cocoa
powder, add the chocolate chips and fold everything in. Leave the
mixture to rest for 20 minutes in the fridge, then roll it out to 5mm thick,
cut to the desired size and bake on a greased baking tray for 15–20
minutes, or until golden brown.

For the beer ice-cream: whip up the eggs and sugar until the mixture
doubles in size. Pour the cream and beer into a pan, bring them to the
boil, then pour the mixture over the egg sabayon. Whip it up again until
cool, churn, then freeze for 12 hours. If you do not have an ice-cream
churn, place it in the freezer, stirring it every hour until ready.

For the chocolate sauce: place half the sugar, the vanilla seeds, the
couverture and 125ml water into a pan and bring them to the boil.
Meanwhile, mix the cornflour, cocoa powder and remaining sugar with a
little water to form a paste. Add this to the boiling chocolate mixture and
cook over a low heat for about 5 minutes until thick, stirring frequently.
Pass the mixture through a sieve and serve either hot or cold.

To serve, arrange a pool of chocolate in the middle of a dish with a cookie
on top. Place a portion of ice-cream on top of this and finish with a
spoonful of whipped cream. Garnish with a sprig of mint and a light
dusting of icing sugar.

Stefano and Julie Bagnoli
Palmiro

Stefano and Julie Bagnoli
Palmiro

Our food is modern Italian – the food that is eaten in Italy today, not a pastiche of 1950s immigrant dishes served with the imagery of grape-crushing peasants.

Palmiro is committed to classical methods of food preparation and uses the best available ingredients to create ever-changing seasonal menus of rustic and fresh flavours. We have tried to reproduce the feeling that you are dining with friends in Stefano's home town of Venice – a place where there is an ingrained food culture, where the days are structured around the rhythm of cooking and eating, and where food, when prepared correctly, is an intense pleasure in itself.

What used to be a car accessories shop near the bohemian suburb of Chorlton has been stripped back into the clean lines of an uncluttered, modernist space, where the focus is firmly on food and where diners find themselves talking between tables, comparing dishes and getting into discussions.

We have chosen dishes that encapsulate our way. Saor is a very traditional Venetian dish which surprises people with its sweet and sour agrodolce flavour – a theme explored in our recipes due to the presence of different vinegars. The Prawns sorrentina uses classic ingredients to bring you the taste of the seaside, while the Pepper liver has a sauce for which you will gladly burn your fingers to taste. And just try the Strawberry crostata for a fresh finish to any meal.

Stefano and Julie Bagnoli
Palmiro

Sarde in saor

with onions in agrodolce

for the sardines

plain flour for dusting
salt and black pepper
50g small sardines, filleted
vegetable oil for deep-frying

for the onions

20g raisins
300ml dry white wine
2 large onions, sliced into half-
rings
1tbsp olive oil
150ml white wine vinegar
1tbsp caster sugar
20g pinenuts, toasted

This dish is best if prepared in advance and left to marinate.

For the sardines: season some flour on a plate, coat the sardine fillets on both sides and set them aside, being careful not to let them stick together. Heat up the oil to a medium heat (about 180°C) and deep-fry the fillets until the bubbles subside or until they are golden in colour. Remove, drain off the oil on some paper, and place them on one side in a dish.

For the onions: soak the raisins in half the white wine for 30 minutes. Fry the onions very gently in olive oil, adding the remaining dry white wine, vinegar and sugar. Cook the onions until they are transparent and all the liquid is absorbed. Add the pinenuts and marinated raisins, and layer the onions and sardines on a dish. Place this in the fridge and leave it to marinade for at least a day before serving.

Prawn sorrentina

with carta da musica bread

for the bread

50g semolina

75g plain flour

1–2tbsp water

a pinch of salt

cornmeal for dusting

for the prawn sorrentina

16 large tiger prawns

3tbsp extra virgin olive oil

3tbsp dry white wine

5 ripe plum tomatoes, roughly chopped

20 black olives, pitted

1tbsp fresh chevril, chopped

salt and pepper

for the garnish

8 fresh basil leaves, deep-fried

For the bread: put all the ingredients in a bowl and mix them into a firm dough. Chill for 1 hour covered with cling film or a brushing of olive oil. Remove from the fridge, remove the cling film and dust the dough with cornmeal. Divide the mixture into 12 balls, then roll them out until paper-thin. Either cook them on a griddle or bake them in a preheated oven (200°C or gas mark 6) for 6–8 minutes until bubbled and crisp. Keep them warm on one side.

For the prawn sorrentina: butterfly the prawns, cutting them down the centre, pulling the sides apart and removing the dark vein. Heat up a frying pan on the full flame, add the oil and drop the heat to a medium temperature. Add the prawns and sear for a minute until pink. Add the white wine, cook off until dry, then add all the other ingredients, leaving the basil until last.

To serve, place the carta da musica bread on a large serving plate and top with the prawns, garnishing with basil leaves and a drizzle of olive oil.

Stefano and Julie Bagnoli
Palmiro

Pepper liver

with Gorgonzola potatoes and balsamic jus

for the Gorgonzola potatoes
150g Gorgonzola cheese
250g double cream
100ml milk
4 large Desirée potatoes, thinly sliced
a knob of unsalted butter

for the pepper liver
1tbsp olive oil
800g veal liver, prepared and in 1cm thick slices
a pinch of crushed black pepper
a pinch of coarse sea salt
200ml light lamb stock
balsamic vinegar
a knob of unsalted butter
red peppercorns to garnish

For the Gorgonzola potatoes: preheat the oven to 220°C (gas mark 6). In a warm pan, break down the cheese with the back of a spoon into the double cream, adding enough milk to make a pouring consistency. Butter or oil a 10cm ring mould and, beginning and ending with potato, pack in alternating layers of potato and the cheese sauce. Top with a knob of butter and bake for 20–30 minutes until golden brown.

For the peppered liver: heat up a frying-pan, add the oil and sear the liver on both sides, sprinkling the coarse salt and pepper into the pan. Cook the meat through to taste (well-done, medium etc.), remove it from the pan and place it on a plate at an angle with the potato.

Pour the stock into the pan, deglaze with a good splash of balsamic vinegar and reduce the liquor be a third. Add a knob of butter and pour the sauce over the liver to serve, garnishing with red peppercorns.

Strawberry crostata

with balsamic jelly

for the jelly
150ml balsamic vinegar
150ml water
300g caster sugar
8 gelatine leaves

for the pastry
150g unsalted butter
150g caster sugar
zest of 1 lemon
330g plain flour
2 large eggs, beaten

for the crostata
700g strawberries
200g caster sugar
70ml water
3 gelatine leaves

For the jelly: boil the balsamic vinegar, water and sugar together until the sugar has dissolved. Take the pan off the heat, add the gelatine, mix until dissolved and pour through a fine sieve into either one large greased mould or four individual ones. Chill for 1½ hours.

For the pastry: cream together the butter and sugar, beat in the lemon zest and flour, and bind the mixture together into a stiff paste with the eggs. Allow it to rest in the fridge for 30 minutes. Preheat the oven to 200°C (gas mark 6). Roll out the pastry to fit a greased, 20cm loose-bottom flan dish, and blind bake in the oven for 10 minutes until golden brown. Remove from the heat.

For the crostata: quarter 500g of the strawberries and arrange them inside the flan dish, working from the centre. Place the sugar, water and remaining strawberries in a pan and boil them down into a syrup before adding the gelatine. Allow this to dissolve, and pass the mixture through a fine sieve. Pour the mixture over the flan and chill in the fridge for 30 minutes.

To serve, press the jelly out of the mould and place it on a dish with a generous slice of crostata.

Mark Bennett
The Malmaison Brasserie

Mark Bennett
The Malmaison Brasserie

I can't tell you exactly how young I was when I first started helping my mother out in the kitchen, but it was certainly very young – young enough for me to be going on a cooking holiday in France at the age of 13 and deciding at that point to become a chef. I qualified at catering college, spent seven tough years training under Bernard Farut at the prestigious Midland Hotel in Manchester, and then landed the dream of a job for a Manchester lad – well, two dream jobs really: running the busy banqueting operations at both Manchester City and Manchester United Football Clubs. Their fixtures rarely clashed because they were in different divisions, so I managed to work alternate shift patterns whilst occasionally getting to watch the teams play.

I worked in various top hotels and restaurants after that, but achieved one of my main ambitions in April 2000: becoming Head Chef at Malmaison – in my home town and before the age of 30 as well. This is an affordable contemporary French brasserie with a multi-cultural twist. We use the best ingredients to produce simple but sophisticated food that is full of character and deep in flavour, and I think the dishes I have chosen here reflect both this and our overall philosophy of food. The simple Sun-blushed tomato and mozzarella salad is a fresh and modern version of a classic starter. The Salmon fish cakes are a Malmaison signature dish – need I say more? – and these are balanced by the sophisticated Risotto nero with baby cuttlefish, which is more of an acquired taste. And, to finish, we have the light and refreshing Pineapple millefeuille with coconut sorbet – a great dessert that also cleanses the palate. I hope you enjoy these dishes and look forward to seeing you at The Malmaison Brasserie.

Mark Bennett
The Malmaison Brasserie

Sun-blushed tomato and mozarella salad

400g buffalo mozzarella
150g sun-blushed tomato quarters
10g fresh purple basil
10g fresh rocket leaves
5ml lime zest and juice
a drizzel of extra virgin olive oil
cracked black pepper

Cut the mozzarella into equal-sized pieces and place them on a cloth to drain off any liquid. Take the tomatoes out of the tub and drain off any oil. Arrange the pieces of mozzarella on the plate and place the sun-blushed tomatoes in between. Arrange the fresh purple basil and rocket leaves on top and drizzle with olive oil and lime juice, seasoning the dish with cracked black pepper.

Risotto nero

with baby cuttlefish

250g baby cuttlefish (whole), cleaned

for the nero stock

25g unsalted butter
25g shallots, chopped
100g fennel, chopped
100g leek, chopped
1 clove of garlic, finely chopped
1 fresh bay leaf
4 black peppercorns
10g fresh tarragon
10g fresh dill
1kg flat-fish bones
20g squid ink
100ml dry white wine
2 litre cold water

for the chilli jam

50g red chilli, de-seeded and finely chopped
30g fresh ginger, finely diced
30g shallots, finely chopped
250g chilli sauce, readymade
250g red onion, finely diced
salt and black pepper

for the risotto

25ml olive oil
125g red onion, finely chopped
1 clove of garlic, finely chopped
10g squid ink
125g carnarol risotto rice
1½ litre nero stock (see above)
25g unsalted butter
salt and black pepper

other ingredients

80g unsalted butter
sprig of chervil to garnish

Much of this dish – like the cuttlefish, chilli jam and stock – can be prepared a couple of days in advance and kept in the fridge until needed.

For the nero stock: melt the butter in a large pan and add the shallots, fennel and leek. Sauté gently for a few minutes before adding the garlic, bay leaf, peppercorns, dill and tarragon. Cover with a lid and cook for 10–15 minutes, stirring occasionally until the vegetables are soft. Add the fish bones, squid ink, white wine and water and bring to the boil, skimming off any surface residue that forms. Simmer for 20 minutes, remove from the heat and strain through a fine sieve. Set the stock aside until ready to use.

For the chilli jam: sweat down the chilli, ginger, shallots and onion in a thick-based pan, without allowing them to brown. Add the chilli sauce and cook it through until the mixture becomes tight. Check the seasoning and allow to cool.

For the baby cuttlefish: remove the tentacles and leave them to one side. Then stuff the cuttlefish with the chilli jam, using cocktail sticks to hold it together, and refrigerate along with the tentacles until needed.

For the risotto: heat the oil in a pan and fry the onions and garlic for a few minutes. Add the squid ink, then the rice and cook for a few more minutes, stirring occasionally. Slowly start adding about 1½ litres of the nero stock, stirring constantly and ensuring that all the liquid has been absorbed before adding more. When the rice is cooked, add the butter and adjust the seasoning and consistency. It should be moist but not too runny. If it is on the runny side, set it aside for a while and let the rice soak up more of the stock. Line a tray with cling film and spread the rice out on top to cool until ready to use.

When ready to serve, melt down the butter in a pan and add the cooked risotto. Heat up a little of the remaining nero stock, slowly add this to the risotto until you have the right consistency, and keep this warm on one side. Pan-fry the cuttlefish and tentacles in olive oil for no more than 5 minutes until cooked. Mould the hot risotto in a large ring on a serving plate, arranging the cuttlefish and tentacles on top. Garnish with a sprig of chervil.

Salmon fish cakes

with parsley sauce and spinach timbales

for the fish cakes

500g salmon fillet, skinned
1 lemon, sliced
salt and black pepper
500g potatoes
200ml tomato ketchup
100ml Tabasco sauce
100ml Worcestershire sauce
200g breadcrumbs

for the fish sauce

50g unsalted butter
25g plain flour
250ml fish stock, warm
50ml double cream
salt and black pepper

for the spinach timbale

200g large leaf spinach
25g unsalted butter
100g flat leaf parsley, chopped

For the fish cakes: poach the salmon for 10 minutes in hot water with a pinch of salt and the sliced lemon. Remove it and leave to cool. Meanwhile, boil the potatoes for 20 minutes and simply drain and mash them. Then mix the salmon and potato together, adding the ketchup, Tabasco and Worcestershire sauce. Check the seasoning, and add breadcrumbs to adjust the consistency until it is fairly tight. Then divide the mixture into 8, mould it into small barrels and place these in the fridge until required.

For the fish sauce: melt the butter in a pan and slowly add the flour to make a roux. Gradually stir in the warm fish stock until the sauce coats the back of the spoon. Then add the double cream, adjust the consistency as necessary and season to taste.

For the spinach timbale: blanch the spinach in salted boiling water and drain. Brush the inside of 4 small ramekin dishes with butter, and then season these with salt and black pepper. Line each with the larger spinach leaves and pack down the rest of the spinach inside. Press out any excess water.

Preheat the oven to 180°C (gas mark 4) and pan-fry the fish cakes in a little olive oil for 1 minute on each side to seal them. Remove the fish cakes from the pan, place them on a baking tray and cook them in the oven for about 5–6 minutes until golden brown. Heat through the sauce, adding the chopped parsley at the end, and warm up the spinach timbale for about 20 seconds in the microwave.

To serve, place two fish cakes in the middle of each plate, with the spinach timbale at the top and fish sauce spooned carefully over.

Mark Bennett
The Malmaison Brasserie

Pineapple millefeuille
with coconut sorbet

for the pineapple
1 large sweet pineapple, peeled
and cored
50g unsalted butter
100g caster sugar

for the sorbet
500ml water
5g glucose
400g caster sugar
250ml coconut purée

for the tuille
75g unsalted butter
125g caster sugar
75g plain flour
75g desiccated coconut
4 egg whites

for the garnish
sprigs of fresh mint
icing sugar for dusting

For the sorbet: boil the water, glucose and sugar together until the sugar is dissolved. Remove from the heat and add the coconut purée. Allow to cool then churn and freeze. (Alternatively, beat the sorbet mixture and place it in the freezer for a few hours, repeating this process regularly over a 24-hour period.)

For the tuille: melt the butter and cool it until it is luke warm. Mix in the sugar, flour and egg whites until the sugar has dissolved, then cover and chill overnight.

Preheat the oven to 180°C (gas mark 4). Slice the pineapple into ½cm rings. Then make a template out of something like a plastic lid – slightly bigger than the sliced pineapple – and spoon some chilled tuille mixture into the centre. Spread it out thinly and evenly, and gently lift it away from the template, repeating this until you have used up all of the mixture. Sprinkle each with some coconut and bake in the oven for 5–6 minutes. Remove when golden and leave to cool.

When ready to serve, pan-fry the pineapple rings in a little unsalted butter and sugar until they are soft and caramel in colour. Allow these to cool. Place a tuille biscuit in the centre of the plate with a pineapple ring on top. Place another biscuit on top, then another ring and finally a biscuit, topping these with a perfect ball of coconut sorbet. Garnish with a sprig of mint and a light dusting of icing sugar, then drizzle some cooking liquor from the pineapple around the plate.

Raymond Blanc
Le Petit Blanc

Raymond Blanc
Le Petit Blanc

Many of my English friends believe that the heart of the French home is the bedroom, but they are mistaken. It is the dining table, where friends and family meet, talk and celebrate. It may sound like a cliché, but that's how I started. I come from a working-class family and my mother's food was born out of poverty. Every ladle of soup delivered to the table was an act of love that tasted delicious.

I first set foot on British soil in 1972 and entered the dark world of catering as a waiter. I was given a nasty little room with no water and £13 a week on which to survive, but then the chef fell ill and I took over. From that moment on I knew my destiny. I became a chef – completely self-taught.

At the time, food was not considered important in Britain and catering was seen as a subservient craft. But I wanted to change all that; I wanted to show that food is good for everyone. In 1977, at the age of 28, I opened my first restaurant, Les Quat' Saisons, in Summer Town, Oxford, where I recreated my mother's cooking. Two years later we got our first Michelin star and, two years after that, our second. Our humble little restaurant had become England's best.

In 1984 my friends helped me to transform a decaying manor house in Great Milton, Oxford, into one of the most beautiful restaurants and country house hotels in Europe – Le Manoir aux Quat' Saisons – fulfilling another long-held dream. However, I had always wanted to create a brasserie in the truest sense of the word – one offering a wide range of simple French food throughout the day and at prices most people could afford. The result was Le Petit Blanc, the first of which opened in Oxford in 1996. In November 2000 we opened in Manchester with a clear aim: to be the city's best. It is a brasserie born out of a culture of welcome and hospitality, and the dishes that follow give you a taste of the fresh and wholesome seasonal cuisine on which we pride ourselves.

Deep-fried
crab cakes

with green onion risotto and chilli salsa

for the crab cakes
300g whiting fillet
2 eggs
salt and ground white pepper
1 red chilli, de-seeded and finely chopped
½tsp ground coriander
½tsp ground fresh ginger (about 1cm root)
a little finely grated lime zest
1 shallot, finely chopped
85 ml double cream
100g white crab meat
plain flour and dry breadcrumbs for coating

for the risotto
1tbsp olive oil
2 shallots, finely chopped
1 clove of garlic, finely chopped
½tsp fresh thyme, chopped
200g risotto rice
400ml hot vegetable stock
2tbsp double cream
100g mascarpone
4 spring onions, chopped
75g Parmesan, grated
salt and black pepper to taste

for the salsa
200g plum tomatoes, skinned, de-seeded and chopped
3 shallots, finely chopped
1 red chilli, de-seeded and finely chopped
1 clove of garlic, crushed

for the mustard vinaigrette
15g white wine vinegar
30g olive oil
5g Dijon mustard

other ingredients
vegetable oil for frying
4 tbsp chilli oil
chervil sprigs to garnish

For the crab cakes: liquidise the whiting with 1 egg in a blender until smooth. Add salt, pepper, chilli, coriander, ginger, lime zest and shallot, then fold in the cream and crab meat. Divide the mixture into four, shape it into round cakes and chill until firm. Then roll the cakes in flour, brush them with the remaining beaten egg and coat them in breadcrumbs. Repeat this, then chill the crab cakes until ready to cook.

For the risotto: heat the oil in a frying pan and fry the shallots, garlic and thyme until soft. Add the rice and cook for 2–3 minutes before pouring on the hot stock. Simmer for 10–15 minutes, stirring frequently, until the rice is tender but still has a little bite. When ready to serve, stir in the cream and reheat. Add the mascarpone, spring onion and Parmesan and check for seasoning.

For the salsa: mix together the vinegar, olive oil and mustard to make the vinaigrette, then add 4tsp of it to the salsa ingredients. Mix everything together and chill.

To serve, deep-fry the crab cakes in hot oil until golden, and drain on kitchen paper. Spoon the hot risotto on to the centre of four serving dishes and place a crab cake on top of each. Spoon a little salsa on each crab cake, and drizzle the chilli oil around the risotto. Garnish with chervil sprigs.

Pan-fried sea bass

with colcannon and coriander dressing

for the coriander dressing

80g fresh coriander, washed

1 clove of garlic, peeled and crushed

10g pine nuts

60g olive oil

1g salt

black pepper to taste

a squeeze of lemon juice

20g Parmesan, freshly grated

for the colcannon

280g new potatoes

80g savoy cabbage, finely shredded

40g pancetta, diced

40g olive oil

40g spring onions, finely sliced

40g sun-dried tomatoes, sliced

2g salt

black pepper to taste

for the sea bass

40g olive oil

40g unsalted butter

4 x 140g fillets of sea bass, or any other fish

4g salt

1g black pepper

for the garnish

40g pancetta

For the coriander dressing: blend the coriander, garlic and pine nuts in a food processor, slowly adding the olive oil. Pour the mixture into a bowl and add the seasoning, lemon juice and grated Parmesan. If the dressing is too thick, add more oil or, if too runny, add more Parmesan.

For the garnish: slice the pancetta very thinly into 1mm strips and cook them in the oven at 180°C (gas mark 4) for 7 minutes. Take them out of oven and leave them to dry on one side for 30 minutes.

For the colcannon: cook the potatoes in salted boiling water for about 20 minutes then crush them roughly. Blanch the savoy cabbage for 2 minutes in boiling water and dry fry the bacon until golden brown. Place the olive oil and crushed potatoes into a pan, cook for about 2 minutes on a low heat, then add the blanched cabbage and cook for a further 3 minutes. Add the bacon lardons, spring onions and sun-dried tomatoes, cook for a further 3–4 minutes until the potatoes are hot, and season to taste.

For the sea bass: heat the butter and olive oil in a frying pan. When foaming, add the fish fillets flesh-side down and cook for 30 seconds. Then turn them over, cook them skin-side down for 3 minutes and season to taste.

Serve on large plates, moulding the colcannon with ring cutters and placing the fish on top. Drizzle the coriander dressing around the edge and finish with the pancetta crisps.

Lamb loin coated in sesame seeds and black pepper

with buttered cabbage, deep-fried carrots and caramelised vegetables

for the lamb

4 x 200g lamb loin
100g sesame seeds
25g crushed black pepper
400g large potatoes
50ml double cream
50g unsalted butter
salted and black pepper to taste

for the lamb jus

1kg lamb bones, chopped into small pieces
50g unsalted butter
100g Spanish onion
100g carrots
100g celery
100g tomato purée
500g plum tomatoes, roughly chopped
4 garlic cloves, peeled and halved
10g fresh rosemary
1g fresh thyme
1 bay leaf
1g whole white peppercorns
1.5 litres water

for the garnishes

12 baby carrots
25g plain flour
1 egg
100g breadcrumbs
300g savoy cabbage
60g butter
salt and black pepper to taste
nutmeg, freshly grated, to taste
12 baby turnips, cut in half
12 baby leeks, cut in half
12 baby fennel, cut in half
25g caster sugar

For the lamb jus: preheat the oven to 200°C (gas mark 6). Place the lamb bones in a roasting dish and roast them in the oven for 15 minutes. Meanwhile, peel and chop the onion, carrots and celery into a 2cm dice and caramelise them in a pan in melted butter – without burning them! When they are ready, drain both the roasted lamb bones and the vegetables and place them in a large pot together. Add the tomato purée and cook over a low heat for 4 minutes. Add all the remaining vegetables and herbs, cook for another 4 minutes, then pour over the water and bring the mixture to the boil. Simmer over a low heat for 1 hour, pass the mixture through a chinoix or fine sieve and reduce the stock rapidly until it has the sauce consistency required. You will need about 120ml to garnish this dish.

For the lamb: preheat the oven to 220°C (gas mark 7). Roll the lamb in the sesame seeds and black pepper, seal it in a hot pan, and roast it in the oven for 10–12 minutes. Boil, drain and mash the potatoes, then add the cream and butter, with seasoning to taste.

For the garnishes: dip the carrots in the flour, then the egg wash and finally the breadcrumbs, and deep-fry them until golden brown. Sweat the cabbage in 30g butter and season with salt, pepper and nutmeg. Caramelise the turnips, leeks and fennel in the remaining butter and the sugar.

To serve, mould the mash with a ring cutter and top with the cabbage. Slice the lamb and place it on top, garnishing with the carrots, caramelised vegetables and lamb jus.

Tarte tatin

with vanilla ice-cream

4 Bramley apples, peeled, cored
and cut in half
40g demerara sugar
30g unsalted butter
240g puff pastry, readymade
160g vanilla ice-cream
20g caramel liquid, readymade

Preheat the oven to 220°C (gas mark 6). Cut four of the apple halves into five segments each and place them in a pan with 30g sugar and 20g butter. Gently cook until golden brown, remove and drain. Add the rest of the apple halves to the same pan, cook for a further 2 minutes until golden brown, remove and drain.

Roll out the puff pastry until it is 1mm thick and cut it into discs using an 8 x 2cm tarte mould. Gently melt the remaining 10g butter, and coat 4 tarte moulds with it using a brush, sprinkling them with the remaining demerara sugar to form a crust. Place the halved apples in the middle of the moulds and layer the segments around and out to the edges, pressing the fruit well down. Place the pastry discs on top, and cook the tartes in the oven for 20 minutes, before turning the heat down to 180°C for a further 10 minutes. Turn each tarte out on to a plate. Serve beside vanilla ice-cream with the caramel liquid poured over the top.

Robert Brown
Lounge 10

Robert Brown
Lounge 10

Over the years I have managed to get quite a reputation for my food. I use simple ingredients as creatively and imaginatively as possible, selecting the freshest produce from suppliers from all over the country and focusing on its flavours, textures and colours. I also make a point of putting each dish together personally for every customer I serve. Indeed, getting everything absolutely right is extremely important to me, so I always take the time to go out and meet our guests, check that everything is to their satisfaction and make sure that everyone – staff included – are relaxed and happy.

Stephen Perks creates all the desserts at Lounge 10. But while you may well hear him shouting out instructions, you'll never see him outside of the kitchen. He too keeps things simple – dishes so delicate, so imaginative that customers have described them as 'orgasmic'.

The result? Since opening in April 2001 Lounge 10 has received innumerable accolades and glowing reports, attracting various celebrities and high-profile diners on a regular basis. Enjoy the dishes that follow – and especially Stephen's to-die-for Crème brûlée.

Sea bass

with fennel and lemon oil

4 x 175g sea bass fillets
1tsp extra virgin olive oil
4 fennel bulbs
16 black olives, pitted
for the garnish
20 sprigs chervil
4 tomatoes, skinned, de-seeded
and diced
30ml olive oil
30ml lemon juice, freshly
squeezed

For the sea bass: cut each fillet in half on the diagonal. Then pan-fry them skin-side down in a little olive oil for 1 minute, turn them over and cook them for a further 2 minutes on the other side. Leave them in a warm place to cook through.

For the fennel: remove the leaves and keep them on one side for the garnish. Blanch the fennel bulbs in boiling salted water for 1 minute, refresh them in iced water and shred them finely. Put the shredded fennel into a sauté pan, cook it in a little olive oil for 1 minute until it is warmed through and add the olives.

To serve, place the fennel mixture in the centre of a plate with the sea bass on top. Stand the fennel leaves up so that they tumble over the fish, and add the tomato concasse around the edge. Then mix the olive oil and lemon juice together to make a lemon oil and drizzle over a few drops, garnishing with the chervil.

Veal and red pepper mash

with a morel sauce

4 x 175g veal cutlets
1tsp olive oil
for the red pepper mash
2 large potatoes, peeled
salt and black pepper
1 red pepper
for the morel sauce
100g fresh morels
½tsp olive oil
50ml Marsala
250ml double cream

For the red pepper mash: heat up the grill until it is very hot. Boil the potatoes until soft, drain them off, and mash them up with salt and black pepper to taste. Keep them warm on one side until required. Meanwhile, grill the pepper until it is blackened and blistered, and either place it in a plastic bag or wrap it in cling film until cool. This will help the skin come off so that you can peel it more easily. Then dice the pepper into chunky pieces and add them to the mash.

For the veal: preheat the oven to 240°C (gas mark 9). Heat the olive oil in an ovenproof pan, add the veal cutlets and seal them on both sides. Then place them in the oven for about 8 minutes. When golden brown, take them out again and leave them to rest in a warm place.

For the morel sauce: sauté the morels in the olive oil. Then pour in the Marsala and reduce the mixture by half. Add the cream and reduce the sauce again until thickened.

To serve, mould the mash using a ring cutter, stand the veal cutlet next to it and finish the dish with the sauce.

Truffle pizza

for the pizza base

15g fresh yeast
250ml tepid water
32ml truffle oil, readymade
15ml tepid milk
125g strong white flour
a pinch of salt

for the topping

1 mozzarella ball, drained and cut
into 16 slices
20 slices fresh truffle
sprigs of chevil to garnish

For the pizza base: mix the yeast, water, truffle oil and milk together and leave them to stand for 5 minutes in a warm place. Add the salt to the flour, sift this into a mixing bowl and make a well in the centre. Pour the yeast mixture in, combine the ingredients and kneed until it forms a dough. Cover the bowl with a clean damp cloth and leave it to rest and prove for about 20 minutes. Once it has risen, knock the dough back, cut it into 4 equal pieces and roll them out into circles, each about 2mm thick.

To cook, place the pizza base under a hot grill for 2 minutes, turn it over and put 4 slices of mozzarella on top. Put it back under the grill until the cheese is warm, then scatter on 5 slices of truffle and warm the pizza through again. Garnish with the chervil and serve.

Crème brûlée

with red fruits and almond tuille

for the almond tuille

50g icing sugar

55g plain flour

45g unsalted butter

3 egg whites

50g ground almond

for the crème brûlée

60g raisins

3 shots of rum

300ml double cream

1 vanilla pod, split with the seeds scraped out

4 egg yolks

30g caster sugar

for the red fruits

½ punnet strawberries

1 punnet raspberries

1 punnet blueberries

½ punnet blackberries

juice of 2 lemons

40g caster sugar

20g fresh ginger, very finely chopped

For the almond tuille: melt the butter and allow it to cool until it is luke warm. Mix it together with all of the remaining ingredients and blitz until smooth, leaving it to cool overnight. Preheat the oven to 220°C (gas mark 7) and line a baking tray with oiled baking paper. Divide the mixture into four, spreading it out thinly into circles. Bake in the oven for 5–6 minutes until golden brown, remove from the heat and peel the biscuits off, moulding them immediately so that they curl. Leave them to cool.

For the crème brûlée: preheat the oven to 180°C (gas mark 4) and place four 9cm ramekin dishes in a tray of water. Then soak the raisins in the rum. Warm the cream with the vanilla pod in a pan until it is just off simmering point – do not let it boil – and leave this to infuse for 5 minutes. Cream the egg yolks and sugar together until they become white and fluffy, and fold this into the cream mixture while it is still warm. Then leave this for about 20 minutes until all the bubbles have settled.

Put a quarter of the raisins into each ramekin and pour over the cream mixture. Bake in the oven for about 30 minutes until lightly set. (Don't be tempted to turn up the oven to speed up the cooking process because the egg will curdle.)

For the red fruits: mix all the fruit together in a bowl and pour over the lemon juice. Add the sugar and ginger and mix everything together again.

To serve, place the crème brûlée on a plate, with the almond tuille on one side and the red fruits carefully spooned around the edge.

James Gingell
Restaurant Bar & Grill

James Gingell
Restaurant Bar & Grill

There were two reasons really why I wanted to become a chef. The main one has got to be my uncle, who owned a restaurant and who I admire greatly. But I also did a lot of travelling when I was young, so between my uncle and a delight in all the different foods I experienced abroad, my fate was sealed.

Since then I have worked in numerous quality country-house hotels around the UK, but the two years I spent in Cape Town, South Africa, and Sydney, Australia, are undoubtedly the most memorable – for obvious reasons. I love working abroad, and my long-term ambition is to own a restaurant and cookery school in Tuscany. That being said, I did return to England, working as Sous Chef at Heathcotes Brasserie, before opening Simply Heathcotes as Head Chef. I then left the restaurant world in order to broaden my outlook, working for a short while as a development chef for Marks and Spencer. But I was lured back again for the opening of the Restaurant Bar and Grill's sister restaurant, Piccolino in Knutsford, and have never looked back since.

I became Executive Chef at the Restaurant Bar and Grill in January 2001. The food here is modern and eclectic – simple, high-quality dishes that use the best ingredients – and you'll find a taste of our approach to food in the pages that follow.

Roasted vine tomatoes

with mozzarella bruschetta

1 ball of buffalo mozzarella
(approx. 200g), cut into 15g slices

for the tomatoes

6 vine tomatoes, sliced in half
lengthways

2g Maldon sea salt

2 cloves of garlic, chopped

2g fresh thyme, picked

50ml extra virgin olive oil

for the bruschetta

8 slices ciabatta bread, 5–8cm
thick

30ml extra virgin olive oil

2g Maldon sea salt

for the balsamic dressing

200ml balsamic vinegar

50ml glucose syrup (or caster
sugar)

for the garnish

8 large basil leaves, unblemished

black pepper

For the tomatoes: preheat the oven to 100°C. Arrange the tomatoes on a metal baking tray and sprinkle them with the sea salt, garlic, thyme and olive oil. Then place them in the oven for about 6 hours so that the tomatoes semi-dry out and their flavour becomes concentrated.

For the bruschetta: this can be made using either a grill pan or in the oven. If using an oven, preheat it to 150°C (gas mark 2). Lightly brush the ciabatta bread with the olive oil, and sprinkle a little sea salt over the top. If using a grill pan, cook the slices on both sides until they have an attractive bar-marking and set them to one side. If using an oven, place the slices on a metal baking tray for about 10–15 minutes until golden brown.

For the balsamic dressing: mix the balsamic vinegar and glucose syrup in a pan and place it on the heat. Reduce the mixture by half until the balsamic becomes thick and syrupy, coating the back of a spoon. Set aside to cool once ready.

For the garnish: these aren't strictly necessary but provide an attractive garnish. Place the basil leaves into the deep-fat fryer and stand back immediately as they will spit. As soon as the spitting stops they are ready, so remove them and place them on kitchen paper to dry.

To prepare the dish, top the tomatoes with the mozzarella and place them under the grill until the cheese is brown and starts bubbling. In the meantime, swirl the reduced balsamic across the plate and place 2 pieces of bruschetta in the centre. Then neatly arrange 3 grilled tomato pieces on the top, and garnish with the deep-fried basil and a twist of black pepper.

Grilled sea bass

with summer vegetables and a herb butter sauce

4 x 130g sea bass fillets, boned and scaled
extra virgin olive oil
5g Maldon sea salt

for the herb butter
100g salted butter
10g flat leaf parsley
15g garlic purée

for the butter sauce
30g shallots, peeled and roughly chopped
60ml dry white wine
60ml white wine vinegar
60ml whipping or double cream
250g unsalted butter, diced and chilled
20g chives, finely chopped
12 fresh basil leaves, torn
20g fresh flat leaf parsley, roughly chopped
salt and white pepper

for the summer vegetables
200g baby carrots
500g medium asparagus
80g broad beans, skinned, cooked and frozen
200g fine green beans, topped and tailed
250g cherry tomatoes, cut in half

For the herb butter: soften the butter and, either with a spoon or a food processor, beat in the parsley and garlic purée. Set this aside in the fridge until required.

For the butter sauce: add the shallots, wine, vinegar and cream to a small pan and reduce the mixture by half. When it becomes thick and syrupy, remove the pan from the heat and slowly start whisking in the butter so that the sauce emulsifies. Then pass it through a fine sieve, discard the shallots and season to taste. Set it aside in a warm place – neither hot nor cold – and serve warm when required.

For the summer vegetables: remove the stalk and leaves from the carrots and peel them as normal, but using a small knife not a peeler. Scrape the carrots in water to remove the peel, and cook them in boiling water for 4–5 minutes. Then remove the tough stalk bases from the asparagus – the last 3–4cm, depending on size. Bring a medium-sized pan of salted water to the boil, and fill a sink or medium-sized container with ice-cold water. Blanch the asparagus for about 4 minutes, then remove it carefully and place it in the cold water. It should be crisp and retain a bright, vibrant green colour. Allow the water to come back up to a rolling boil again, then add the green beans for 2–3 minutes, repeating the same process as for the asparagus. Then remove the vegetables from the iced water and set them aside. Cut the asparagus in half, keeping the tips for a garnish and cutting the remainder into rounds. Make sure no tough outer skins remain on the broad beans.

For the sea bass: make small incisions into the skin from the top to the tail, ensuring that you don't cut through the fillet. Then place it in the fridge until required. A couple of minutes before cooking, remove the fish and sprinkle them with sea salt. This helps to crisp up the skin and improves final presentation. Preheat the oven to 200°C (gas mark 6), and heat up 1tbsp olive oil in an oven proof frying pan. Place the fillets skin-side down in the pan for about 1–2 minutes until the skin is crispy, and, without turning them over, place them in the oven and cook for 8–10 minutes.

Meanwhile, slowly melt the herb butter in a pan, making sure that it does not colour. Add the baby carrots, sautéing them for 2 minutes, then the fine green beans, sautéing for another 2 minutes and then the asparagus tips for a further 2 minutes. Next add the broad beans, and the rest of the asparagus, mixing carefully without too much heat. Finally add the cherry tomatoes, and set the dish aside in a warm place until ready for plating.

To prepare the dish, place the vegetables in the centre of the plate, with the crisp-skinned sea bass on top. Mix the chives, basil and parsley into the butter sauce, and spoon this around, before drizzling a small amount of extra virgin olive oil over.

Baked salmon

with roasted artichokes, new potatoes and salsa verde

for the tomato vinaigrette

100g vine tomatoes

10g onion, chopped

50ml extra virgin olive oil

15ml white wine vinegar

5g tomato purée

5g fresh basil

5g fresh tarragon

2g salt

1g black pepper

2g fennel seeds

2g caraway

4g garlic, whole (1–2 cloves, depending on size)

for the salsa verde

75ml extra virgin olive oil

60g capers

40g flat leaf parsley, picked

15g anchovies, in oil

10g garlic, whole (3–4 cloves, depending on size)

10g Dijon mustard

for the salmon

4 x 200g salmon fillets

1tbsp extra virgin olive oil

6g Maldon sea salt

other ingredients

1tbsp extra virgin olive oil

250g artichokes, marinated and quartered

320g new potatoes, quartered and boiled

60g cherry tomatoes, halved

20g fresh flat leaf parsley, roughly chopped

for the garnish

8 basil leaves, unblemished

12 caper berries

For the tomato vinaigrette: put all the ingredients in a saucepan and simmer slowly over a low heat for about 10–12 minutes until the tomatoes have broken down and the onion has softened. Remove the mixture from the heat, and blitz it in a food processor until it is a smooth, emulsified liquid purée. Pass the mixture through a fine sieve and set it aside until required. (You can make this well in advance.)

For the salsa verde: blitz all the ingredients to a fine paste in a food processor, and refrigerate until required. (You can make this well in advance.)

For the garnish: place the basil leaves into the deep-fat fryer and stand back immediately as they will spit. As soon as the spitting stops they are ready, so remove them and place them on kitchen paper to dry.

For the salmon: try to buy salmon fillets with the skin intact as this helps the presentation of the dish. Preheat the oven to 200°C (gas mark 6), and heat up the olive oil in an oven proof frying pan. Lightly sprinkle the fillets with sea salt and place them skin-side down in the pan for about 2–3 minutes until the skin is crispy. Without turning the fillets over, place them in the oven and cook for 10–15 minutes until the salmon is golden on top but still slightly moist inside.

For the vegetables: heat up a frying pan on a medium heat and add the olive oil. Then add the potatoes and start colouring them lightly for about 4–5 minutes, before adding the artichokes, shortly followed by the cherry tomatoes and parsley. By this time the salmon should be almost ready and the potato mixture lightly coloured.

To prepare the dish, place the potato mixture in the centre of the plate with the salmon skin-side up on top. Garnish the top with a spoonful of salsa verde and 2 deep-fried basil leaves, then drizzle some tomato vinaigrette and a little extra virgin olive oil around the edge. Add 3 caper berries and sprinkle with a little more sea salt to serve.

Panacotta

with berry compote and biscotti

for the panacotta
600ml whipping cream
70g caster sugar
2 vanilla pods, split
lengthways
1½ gelatine leaves, bronze

for the berry compote
200g blackberries, frozen
200g strawberries, frozen
80g caster sugar
juice of ½ lemon

for the biscotti
100g strong baking flour
140g caster sugar
100g pistachio kernels,
shelled and roughly
chopped
zest of 2 lemons, grated
3g baking powder
2 egg yolks
1 egg white

For the panacotta: it is important to have the correct moulds for this dish – ideally 120ml aluminium dariole moulds. Pour the cream and sugar into a pan, add the vanilla pods, and bring this to a slow, constant simmer for 5 minutes, stirring occasionally to disperse the vanilla seeds and their flavour. Meanwhile, soften the gelatine in a little cold water, then wring out any excess. Remove the cream from the heat, and stir in the softened gelatine until it is totally dissolved throughout the mixture. Pass this through a fine sieve into a clean bowl or jug and discard the vanilla pods. Then pour the cream mixture into the moulds and refrigerate over night, or for at least 8 hours before serving.

For the berry compote: for consistency's sake, we actually use frozen berries for this recipe – with a few fresh ones for garnishing – as the price of fresh berries fluctuates so widely throughout the year. Heat up a large-based saucepan until it is scalding hot. Add the berries, which will immediately begin to break down. Add the sugar and lemon juice, and stir constantly as the mixture continues to break down. When all the juice is extracted from the berries and the liquid begins to bubble, remove it from the heat, allow it to cool and then refrigerate until required.

For the biscotti: mix together the flour, 100g sugar, nuts, lemon zest and baking powder in a large bowl so that the nuts are evenly distributed throughout. Make a well in the centre and combine the egg yolks into a dough. If it is slightly wet, add a touch more flour so that the mixture is easier to work with. Roll the dough into a thick sausage shape on a floured surface, transfer it to a metal tray and refrigerate for 1–2 hours.

Preheat the oven to 180°C (gas mark 4) and remove the dough from the fridge. Brush the surface with a little egg white, sprinkle it evenly with a little extra caster sugar, then bake it in the oven for 1 hour – checking it every 20 minutes. Treat the biscotti like a cake. The outside will be golden brown and crispy and the inside will be soft but cooked – a good test being to slide a clean knife into the centre and checking to see if it is still clean when it comes out again. When the biscotti is ready, remove it from the oven and set it on one side to cool. Turn the oven down to 50°C. When the biscotti is cooled but still a little warm, cut it into wafer-thin slices, lay them on to a baking tray and place them in the oven for another hour to dry out.

To serve, remove the panacotta from the fridge and, one at a time, dip each mould into hot water for 10 seconds. The panacotta should slide out intact. Place it in the centre of the plate, spoon the berry compote around the edge, and garnish it with a few fresh berries. To finish, place a biscotti on the top.

Patrick Hannity
The Lime Tree

Patrick Hannity
The Lime Tree

Unfulfilled by the prospect of a career in marketing, I gave up my job in 1985 to travel around America. Three months later, short of money and desperate for work, I ended up in the kitchens of one of New Orleans' top restaurants. This is where my love affair with restaurants really began.

I have had no formal training as a chef, but an interest in cooking and good quality food was instilled in me at home in Belfast by my mother, who is a great home cook, and my father, who was a butcher. So just two years after hitting the road in the States I opened The Lime Tree – on a shoestring, with a business partner and a handful of staff, some of whom are still working with us today. Indeed, it is the excellent team of loyal kitchen and front-of-house staff who have helped to maintain the restaurant's standards and reputation, in the face of stiff competition from Manchester's growing restaurant scene.

I have been sole owner of The Lime Tree since 1995 and believe that a hands-on approach is critical to the style and success of the restaurant. I am passionate about the food that we serve. We rely heavily on the quality and seasonal availability of our raw produce, trying to source these locally and using organic wherever possible. The dishes chosen here are representative of the Lime Tree style: natural and honest rather than fussy and over-elaborate – food that has attracted a regular clientèle, critical acclaim and media attention without us ever having to advertise.

Grilled asparagus spears

with sweet roasted peppers, goats cheese
and basil dressing

16 spears of jumbo asparagus*
4 red peppers
4 medium slices goats cheese
salt and black pepper
olive oil
green and red basil pesto, thinned
out with vinaigrette to pouring
consistency

Blanch the asparagus in lots of boiling water, leave until slightly undercooked and refresh in iced water. Grill the peppers until black and blistered, remove them from the heat and wrap them in cling film. This will continue the cooking process to ensure they are sweet and tender. When cool, peel off the skins and slice thickly.

Arrange the asparagus spears on a tray in groups of 4. Season lightly with salt and pepper and then top with slices of the pepper and goats cheese. Drizzle with a little olive oil and grill until the goats cheese is golden brown and melted. Garnish with the basil pesto dressing and serve.

*NOTE: Asparagus varies greatly in size so try to buy English asparagus during its short but exciting season in May/June. Some coarse asparagus will need to be trimmed around the base of the stalk using a potato peeler before blanching.

Fillets of lemon sole with smoked salmon and spinach

served with tarragon butter sauce

500g fresh baby spinach*
15g unsalted butter, melted
4 x 250g fillets of lemon sole,
skinned and checked for small
bones
8 slices smoked salmon
2 shallots, finely chopped
250ml dry white wine
salt and black pepper
fresh nutmeg to season
for the butter sauce
100ml double cream
200g unsalted butter, diced and
chilled
50g fresh tarragon or herbs
salt and black pepper
other ingredients
1tsp vinaigrette, readymade
16 new potatoes

Preheat the oven to 220°C (gas mark 7). Blanch three-quarters of the spinach in boiling water for 30 seconds and refresh in iced water. Chop it up, season with salt, pepper and a little nutmeg and add the melted butter.

Lay the lemon sole fillets out, skinned side upwards, and top each with two slices of smoked salmon and a quarter of the cooked spinach. Roll them up from the thinnest end and cut each fillet into two 'paupiettes'. Poach these with the shallots and white wine for 7–10 minutes in a shallow dish covered with tin foil in the oven.

For the butter sauce: take the liquid from the poached sole fillets and reduce by two-thirds. Add the cream, bring it back to the boil and gradually whisk in the butter. Add the herbs at the last minute and season to taste.

Dress the remaining spinach with some vinaigrette and arrange it on a plate. Place the lemon sole paupiettes on top and pour the sauce over, serving with some new potatoes.

*NOTE: Ring the seasonal changes with this dish by using sampire, asparagus or fennel instead of spinach.

Roast loin of venison

with root vegetable mash, sweet and sour
red cabbage and port jus

4 x 200g venison loin, off the bone
and well trimmed (save all bones
for the port jus)
salt and black pepper

for the mash
200g potatoes, peeled and
chopped
100g celeriac, peeled and
chopped
100g carrots, peeled and
chopped
100g parsnips, peeled and
chopped
80g unsalted butter
salt and black pepper

for the cabbage
75g soft brown sugar
75ml red wine vinegar
100ml apple juice
1 red cabbage, finely shredded
2 Granny Smith apples, peeled
and chopped
1 small red onion, finely chopped

for the port jus
400ml venison stock
400ml veal stock
250ml red wine
100ml port
10g fresh thyme

For the root vegetable mash: a little bit of work is needed in this dish –
all the vegetables need to be peeled, cooked and puréed separately
using a hand masher or vegetable Mouli. Season each to taste, finish with
a little butter and then layer 4 stainless-steel rings with the different
flavours. These can be reheated in the oven whilst the venison is
cooking.

For the cabbage: combine the sugar and vinegar in a pan and reduce
by three-quarters to a syrup. Add the apple juice and the rest of the
ingredients, cover and cook slowly on a low heat until the apple and
cabbage are tender and all of the liquor has been soaked up.

For the port jus: roast off the vegetables and venison bones, then
combine all of the ingredients in a large saucepan, bring them to the boil
and reduce by three-quarters until the liquid is the right consistency for
a sauce.

For the venison: preheat the oven to 240°C (gas mark 9). Season the
venison portions and seal all of the sides in a hot ovenproof pan. Finish
cooking them in a hot oven for 7–10 minutes, ensuring that the meat is
served pink, then allow them to rest for about 5 minutes. Reheat the mash
and cabbage and present them in the centre of the plate. Slice the
venison and serve it on top of the cabbage, with the port jus around the
edge.

Chocolate and hazelnut cheesecake

with Baileys

for the base

100g sweetened digestive biscuits, crushed

60g unsalted butter

15g soft brown sugar

50g hazelnuts, roasted, peeled and chopped

for the cheesecake

225g dark chocolate

25g caster sugar

175g full fat soft cheese

30ml Baileys Irish Cream

225ml double cream, semi-whipped

for the garnish

whipped cream

One of the beauties of this dish is its simplicity and the fact that you can prepare it a couple of days in advance. The quantities given will easily make enough for 8 people. Don't skimp – you will eat it all!

For the base: melt the butter and sugar together in a pan, then add the chopped hazelnuts and crushed biscuits. Press the mixture into the bottom of 7.5cm ring moulds to a depth of about 1cm.

For the cheesecake: melt the chocolate over a pan of simmering water. Meanwhile, beat the sugar and soft cheese until smooth. Slightly cool the chocolate, then mix in the Baileys and cheese mixture, and fold in the cream. Pour into the rings and refrigerate.

We present this dish with coffee anglaise and chocolate sauce, but a dollop of whipped cream is easily enough.

The Kim family
The Koreana

The Kim family
The Koreana

What's Korean food like? Try it and see. For the past 15 years we've been showing people that, although it's similar to Japanese and Chinese cuisine, Korean food has a unique style and taste of its own. This is based on diverse combinations of ingredients like sesame, ginger, chilli, garlic and soy to provide a wide range of fascinating flavours on your palate.

Ours was the first Korean restaurant outside of London and we chose Manchester because we felt that it was the only city with enough good ethnic restaurants already there to allow us to be successful. It opened in 1985, with Alex Kim in front of house and Hyun Kim – drawing on her experiences from Korea where her parents ran a thriving banqueting resort – supervising in the kitchen as Head Chef.

The Koreana flourished until the bombing in the 1990s and, were it not for the sheer number of loyal regular customers, we would not have survived the lean years that followed. But the restaurant was refurbished in 1998 and we have gone from strength to strength. Chul-soo Hong was recruited from Korea as Head Chef to allow Hyun to oversee operations as Executive Chef and our son Jon has taken over in front. We still have the same simple aim that we had when we first opened: to serve high-quality tasty food that is accessible to people in a relaxed and friendly environment. Now, however, with Chul-soo on board, those traditional qualities and flavours are combined with the style and flair of the new to bring you a truly memorable Korean eating experience.

Prawn and spring onion pancakes

with a soy dip

for the dip

1tsp caster sugar
½tsp fresh ginger, minced
½tsp fresh garlic, minced
5tbsp light soy sauce
5tbsp vegetable or chicken stock, warm
½tsp spring onion, finely chopped
½tsp sesame seeds

for the pancake

2 eggs
180g plain flour
80g glutinous rice powder
a large pinch of salt
200ml vegetable or chicken stock, warm
15g red pepper, sliced into thin strips
100g spring onions, sliced lengthways and cut into 8cm strips
70g small prawns
vegetable oil

For the dip: add the sugar, ginger, garlic and soy sauce to the stock, mix thoroughly and allow it to cool. Sprinkle on the spring onion and sesame seeds.

For the pancakes: mix the egg with the plain flour, glutinous rice powder, salt and stock and whisk into a smooth batter. Add a little oil to a 12cm frying pan and warm it on a low–medium heat. Pour in enough batter to cover the base of the pan to a depth of 5mm. Place the red pepper and spring onion in a criss-cross pattern on the upper surface of the pancake, and embed the prawns into it before the batter sets. Turn the pancake over when the underside is crispy and brown, adding more oil if required. When thoroughly cooked, flip it over again, cut it into sections and serve with the soy dip.

Bulgogi

Korean barbecue chicken

for the marinade

40g onion, roughly chopped
160g Mooli radish, roughly chopped
40g pear, cored
20g caster sugar
40ml chicken stock
200ml light soy sauce
100ml rice wine
12g fresh garlic, ground
4g black pepper

for the chicken

800g chicken breast
1 spring onion, thickly sliced
½ tsp sesame seeds
10ml sesame oil
4 shiitake mushrooms, sliced thickly
1 small onion, thickly sliced (optional)

other ingredients

4 cups short-grain white rice
flat-leaf lettuce leaves

For the marinade: purée the onion, radish and pear in a blender. Dissolve the sugar in the chicken stock, then add the soy sauce, rice wine, ground garlic and black pepper. Add this to the purée and mix thoroughly.

For the chicken: cut the chicken into thin slices (3–5mm) – more easily done if it is semi-frozen – and marinade them in the fridge for 1 hour. Add the spring onion, sesame seeds and sesame oil, together with the mushrooms and onion (optional). Then cook the chicken for a few minutes on both sides using a hot griddle pan or, even better, on a charcoal barbecue. Boil the rice in 6–7 cups of water until cooked and sticky.

Serve in a lettuce wrap – using lettuce leaves as the base, topped with a bit of rice and meat and then wrapped up.

Bibim bab

speciality rice with egg, beef and vegetables

4 cups short-grain white rice
160g baby spinach
1 spring onion, finely chopped
2–3 cloves of garlic, minced
1tsp salt
1tsp sesame seeds
160g beansprouts
2tsp sesame oil
160g carrots, shredded or finely sliced
4tsp vegetable oil
160g courgettes, finely sliced
200g beef, thinly sliced
4 medium eggs
160g Mooli radish, shredded or sliced into thin strips
$\frac{1}{2}$tsp chilli powder
1tsp white wine vinegar
1tsp caster sugar
$\frac{1}{4}$tsp fresh ginger, ground or minced
large pinch of salt
1tsp chilli sauce (any variety)

Steam the spinach for about 5 minutes and allow to cool. Season with $\frac{1}{2}$tsp spring onion, $\frac{1}{4}$tsp minced garlic, $\frac{1}{4}$tsp salt and $\frac{1}{2}$tsp sesame seeds, and keep in the fridge until required. Steam the beansprouts for about 5 minutes and allow to cool. Season as for the spinach, but also add 1tsp sesame oil. Mix the carrots with a touch of garlic and salt, shallow fry them in a little vegetable oil until just cooked, and keep them warm. Do the same with the courgettes. Do the same with the beef as well, but fry it using 1tsp sesame oil and 1tsp vegetable oil. Shallow fry 4 eggs until the egg white is cooked, but the yolk is still runny.

Mix together the radish, chilli powder, vinegar, sugar, ginger and salt, and leave on one side for 1 hour.

Place 4 empty ovenproof bowls (earthenware or similar) in a preheated oven at 190°C (gas mark 5) for 15 minutes. (If not available, use any deep bowl to serve the dish in, and ignore the oven instructions.) Cook the rice – 1 part rice to1$\frac{1}{2}$ parts water.

To serve, remove the bowls from the oven using gloves and add the rice. Place an egg centrally in each, sunny-side up, and arrange the previously prepared meat and vegetables radially around the edge. Serve with a teaspoonful of chilli sauce.

To eat, mix the contents of the bowl thoroughly and enjoy. Be careful as the bowls will be hot – you may need to use a heatproof mat.

Orange fritters

with ginger and lemon sauce

for the sauce
4tbsp golden syrup
1tsp fresh ginger, minced
zest and juice of 1 lemon
zest and juice of 1 orange
for the orange fritters
50g plain flour
50g self raising flour
50g cornflour
120ml sparkling mineral water,
ice-cold
3 oranges, peeled and segmented
vegetable oil for frying
vanilla ice-cream

For the sauce: place the syrup, ginger and juice and zest from the lemon and orange in a saucepan and stir over a low heat for 5 minutes, making sure that it does not boil over. Remove from the heat and allow to cool for 1 hour. Pass through a fine sieve into a separate container, and keep on one side until required.

For the orange fritters: place the plain flour, self-raising flour and cornflour in a bowl and slowly stir in the ice-cold mineral water. Coat the orange segments in a little cornflour, dip them in the batter, and deep-fry them in the oil at 180°C until crisp and light brown.

To serve, reheat the syrup, pour it over the fritters and serve with a scoop of ice-cream.

Robert Kisby
Charles Hallé Restaurant
at Bridgewater Hall

Robert Kisby
Charles Hallé Restaurant at Bridgewater Hall

It was only natural that a building of the magnitude of Manchester's £42 million International Concert Hall would provide the platform for the right chef to deliver cuisine to match the quality of the world-famous musicians who play in the auditorium. I am proud that it was me and I have made it my own.

I joined the Bridgewater team shortly after the building opened in September 1996, opening the Charles Hallé Restaurant in the November and developing a renowned menu in the Stalls Café over the years. Indeed, the Bridgewater Hall has allowed me to realise an ambition: to provide some of the best food in Manchester and become one of the city's top chefs.

I strongly believe in leading by example and am constantly excited by what my young brigade and I are able to achieve. I try to take a modern approach to the job, using new technology and systems to take the stress out of the service – well, as much as possible anyway! Likewise, our cuisine is modern in style but based solidly on classical foundations. Only the best ingredients are used – whatever the price – because my priority isn't to spend time making poor produce good but to develop dishes that deliver to the eye and then fulfil that expectation on the palate.

I have gained much personal recognition over the years, but winning *Life* magazine's Manchester Restaurant of the Year 1999/2000 for our work here in the Charles Hallé Room is undoubtedly a high point. And a taste of the quality and care that go into every dish can be found in the pages that follow.

Robert Kisby
Bridgewater Hall

Duck and black pudding rösti

with roasted shallots and a brandy cream sauce

2 Goosenargh duck breasts
250g horseshoe black pudding
for the shallots
100g shallots, peeled
1tbsp olive oil
for the rösti
500g potato, grated
100g celeriac, grated
100g green leek julienne
250ml olive oil
100g clarified butter
salt and black pepper
for the sauce
50g shallots, finely chopped
fresh ginger, finely chopped, to taste
1 clove of garlic, crushed
1 sprig of fresh thyme, finely chopped
50ml brandy
25g unsalted butter
50ml veal glaze
1 bay leaf
200ml reduced brown chicken stock
100ml double cream
salt and black pepper
for the apples
2 Braeburn apples
1tbsp demerara sugar
25g unsalted butter
for the garnish
25g fresh ginger, finely shredded and deep-fried
25g fresh chervil

For the shallots: preheat the oven to 200°C (gas mark 6), then roast the shallots in the olive oil for about 20 minutes until golden brown.

For the rösti: these can be made in advance and reheated when required. Mix together the potato, celeriac and leeks and season to taste. Mould the mixture with an 8cm ring cutter into 12 thin cakes and fry them in the olive oil and clarified butter for about 7 minutes on each side.

For the sauce: sweat off the shallots, ginger, garlic and thyme in a little butter, then flame with the brandy, add the veal glaze and bay leaf and pour in the reduced chicken stock. Bring the mixture to the boil and reduce by a third, before adding the cream, seasoning the sauce to taste and passing it through a fine sieve. Keep the sauce warm until required.

For the duck: trim off any excess fat and score both duck breasts in a criss-cross pattern. Cook them, skin-side down, for 7–8 minutes in a hot pan until golden brown and crisp, then turn them over and continue cooking for as long as required. When ready, remove from the heat and allow them to rest for 10 minutes. Cut up the black pudding into ½cm thick slices. Once rested, return the duck to the pan, skin-side down, and fry it off again until crispy, adding the black pudding for the last minute and sautéing the slices for 30 seconds on each side.

For the apples: cut the apples into 6 pieces each, remove the core and trim the segments into oval or barrel shapes. Melt the butter and sugar in a pan and caramelise the apples for 2 minutes over a medium heat.

To serve, layer up the röstis, black pudding and sliced roasted duck in the centre of a dish, with the apple pieces and shallots arranged around the edge. Carefully spoon the sauce around and garnish with the deep-fried ginger and chervil.

Robert Kisby
Bridgewater Hall

Pan-roasted sea bass fillet

with basil vin blanc sauce and cassoulet with green
vegetables and fresh herbs

for the cassoulet

100g macédoine made from onion,
carrot, leek, celery and fennel
1tbsp olive oil
2 cloves of garlic, crushed
1 sprig of fresh rosemary
1 sprig of fresh thyme
1tbsp tomato purée
200g haricot blanc, soaked overnight
1½ litre chicken or vegetable stock
1tsp mignonette pepper
1 bay leaf
salt to taste
100gm green vegetables, finely diced
(haricot vert, courgette, green leek tops
and small broccoli florets)
mixed fresh herbs, chopped (chervil,
chives, basil, tarragon, flat-leaf parsley
and dill)
25g unsalted butter
salt and black pepper

for the fish

2 x 800g sea bass, scaled, filleted and
pin boned (ask the fishmonger)
6 king scallops
2tbsp olive oil
50g plain flour
25g butter
salt and black pepper

for the sauce

20g unsalted butter
50g white mirepoix
300ml dry white wine
1 litre fish stock
300ml double cream
15g fresh basil, shredded

For the cassoulet: preheat the oven to 180°C (gas mark 4). Pour
the olive oil into a large lidded casserole dish and sweat down the
macédoine, garlic and fresh herb stalks for 5 minutes. Add the
tomato purée, haricot beans and stock and bring the mixture to
the boil. Skim off the surface and add the mignonette pepper and
bay leaf, before putting the lid on and braising the dish in the oven
for about 1¾ hours, stirring occasionally. Add the salt about
three-quarters of the way through the cooking time – not before,
or the beans do not cook properly. When cooked, all the liquor
should be absorbed. Remove the bay leaf and herb sprigs and
allow to cool. Blanch and refresh the mixed vegetables and
broccoli and add them, along with the freshly chopped herbs and
butter, to the beans. Check the seasoning. Cool thoroughly,
keeping it in the fridge until needed.

For the fish: trim the sea bass so that you have nice clean edges.
Clean the scallops thoroughly but do not over-wash them or they
will lose all their flavour. Dry them immediately with kitchen
paper. Then cut each scallop in half lengthways and remove the
corals, keeping these on one side. Place all the fish in the fridge
until needed.

For the sauce: melt half the butter in a pan and sweat down the
mirepoix for about 5 minutes. Add the white wine, bring the
mixture to the boil and reduce by half, then pour in the stock and
reduce by half again, skimming constantly. Add the double
cream, reduce the mixture to a sauce consistency and season to
taste. Pass it through a muslin or fine sieve and set it aside.

To prepare the dish, gently warm the cassoulet through in a
saucepan, stirring from time to time. Meanwhile, lightly flour and
season the sea bass fillets. Heat the olive oil in a large frying pan,
and place the fillets skin-side down first, cooking for 3–4 minutes
on each side. Then caramelise the scallops and coral in a knob of
butter in a red-hot sauté pan for about a minute on each side,
depending on size. Bring the sauce back to the boil, whisk in the
remaining butter and add the shredded basil.

To serve, mould the cassoulet in a 6cm ring and place on a plate,
topping with the sea bass fillet. Arrange 3 half-scallops and the
coral around the edge, surround with a cordon of sauce and
garnish with a fresh basil pluche.

Robert Kisby
Bridgewater Hall

Burgundy-style grilled rib-eye steak

with watercress and seared tomato salad

2kg small rib of beef (on bone)

for the marinade
200ml burgundy
100g macédoine, made from onion, carrot, celery and leek
2 cloves of garlic, crushed
1 bay leaf
2–3 sprigs fresh thyme
1tsp mignonette black pepper

for the stock
100g vegetable mirepoix
1tbsp olive oil
1tbsp tomato purée
1 bouquet garni

for the shallot butter
100g shallots, finely chopped
200ml burgundy
100g unsalted butter
10g flat-leaf parsley, finely chopped
salt and black pepper

for the bourguignon garnish
1tbsp tomato purée
1tbsp plain flour
200ml burgundy
25g smoked bacon lardons
50g baby button mushroom
1tbsp olive oil
4 large savoy cabbage leaves

other ingredients
2 bunches fresh watercress, washed and dried
4 plum tomatoes, halved
25ml olive oil
vinaigrette dressing, readymade
flat-leaf parsley to garnish
Maris Piper potatoes

Prepare the beef 24 hours in advance.

For the rib-eye steak: remove the meat from the bones, separate the eye from the flank and set the bones aside in the fridge. Cut the eye into four 180–200g steaks, trim them and refrigerate. Then cut the flank into a ½cm dice and marinate them in the fridge for 24 hours in the burgundy together with the vegetable macédoine, garlic, bay leaf, thyme and mignonette pepper. Keep any trimmings from the meat with the bones in the fridge over night.

For the stock: next day, roast off the bones and the meat trimmings in a baking tray. Then fry off the mirepoix and tomato purée for about 5 minutes in a little olive oil, add the roasted bones, meat trimmings and bouquet garni and cover with water. Bring this to the boil, skim off the surface and simmer for 1½–2 hours, passing the stock through a fine sieve when it is cooked.

For the shallot butter: peel and finely chop the shallots (place the trimmings in the stock), and sweat these off in a little butter. Add the burgundy, bring this to the boil and reduce it to a syrup, leaving the shallot mixture to cool. Soften the butter, add the parsley, and beat them together with the red wine shallots. Check the seasoning, place the mixture on butter paper, and roll it into a cylinder-shape. Place it in the fridge until firm enough to slice.

For the bourguignon garnish: preheat the oven to 160°C (gas mark 3). Drain the diced meat and macédoine vegetables – reserving the marinade – and fry them off in a hot pan for 5–7 minutes. Transfer them to a casserole dish and stir in the tomato purée, flour, marinade and remaining burgundy, covering with the beef stock. Braise in the oven for about 50 minutes. When the stew is ready, fry off the bacon and mushrooms for 2–3 minutes, spoon out the meat and vegetables from the ragout liquor, and stir them into the bacon mixture. Strain the liquor through muslin or a fine sieve, checking the seasoning. Add enough to the bourguignon mixture to bind it together, and set the remainder aside.

To finish, butter and season four ramekin dishes. Blanch the cabbage leaves for about 1 minute in salted water and refresh them before drying them on kitchen paper. Use them to line the ramekins, allowing the leaves to overlap the edges. Fill each with the bourguignon mix, fold the leaves over the top and press them down.

To prepare the dish, griddle the rib eye steaks to your liking. Sear the tomatoes in a little hot oil, warm through the bourguignon garnish and toss the watercress salad in a little vinaigrette. Place a steak and garnish on each plate, along with some salad topped with two tomato halves. Reheat the remaining ragout sauce and carefully drizzle this around the edge. Slice the butter into 8 thin slices, placing 2 on each steak and garnish with the flat-leaf parsley. Serve with crispy thick chips.

Robert Kisby
Bridgewater Hall

Lemon crème sablé

with fresh raspberries

for the lemon crème

250ml milk
½ vanilla pod, sliced with the
seeds removed
1 large egg
40g caster sugar
40g plain flour
15g cornflour
zest and juice of 1 lemon
125ml double cream
Boyajian pure lemon oil (optional)

for the sablé

200g unsalted butter
100g icing sugar
vanilla essence
2 egg yolks, beaten
250g plain flour

for the coulis

100g raspberries
25g icing sugar
stock syrup

other ingredients

1 punnet fresh raspberries

For the lemon crème: bring the milk and vanilla pod to the boil. The milk should be extremely fresh to ensure that it does not split. Meanwhile, cream the egg and sugar together and stir in the sifted flour and cornflour. Let down the batter with the lemon zest and juice. Pour in the hot milk, beat well and return the lemon mixture to the heat in a clean pan, bringing it back to the boil and stirring continuously for a further 30 seconds. Then place it in a clean bowl, sprinkle the top with a little more caster sugar and cool quickly. Whisk up the double cream until it is stiff. When cold, combine the lemon mixture with the whipped cream and check the flavourings. Should you need to increase the lemon flavour, add a few drops of Boyajian pure lemon oil.

For the sablé: preheat the oven to 200°C (gas mark 6). Cream together the butter, icing sugar and a couple of drops of vanilla essence until pale in colour. Add the egg yolks, then fold in the sifted flour, bringing it together and making it into a disc shape. Leave it to rest in the fridge. Roll it out thinly and cut out the biscuits. Bake in the oven for 10 minutes until lightly golden

For the coulis: blend the raspberries and icing sugar together and pass them through a fine sieve. Use stock syrup to acheive the desired consistency.

To serve, place a biscuit on the plate and pipe the lemon crème over the top. Top this with fresh raspberries and repeat to build up a gateau. Dust with a little icing sugar and accompany with a couple more raspberries and a little coulis.

Paul Kitching
The Juniper

Paul Kitching
Juniper

I started cooking at Juniper when it opened in December 1995. Although I am a self-taught chef, just a few short years later I am now the owner of one of the most prestigious restaurants in Manchester – no mean feat, considering the recent explosion of new restaurants in the city.

Juniper had two main aims when it opened: to build up a loyal core of regular guests who enjoy fine dining; and to achieve critical success and a national reputation. We knew we were getting things right when we were awarded a Michelin star in 1997 – to this day the only one awarded in the Manchester area – and were rated as the city's best restaurant in both the *Good Food* and AA guides. As for the regulars? Well, I'd book well in advance if I were you.

Complacent we are definitely not, however. After five years of undoubted success, we did something radical. We decided to close the restaurant and start again from scratch – a top-to-toe refurbishment so that we could enhance our reputation even further. Out went all the old methods and techniques in the kitchen and in came a totally new approach to cooking. We cook French food – very modern French food – and our philosophy is simple: there should be a balance to every dish. The ones I've chosen for this book reflect my style of cooking and presentation, with flavour – as always – being paramount. Do not be put off by their seeming complexity, though. If you do have any difficulties, give us a ring or visit the restaurant and I'll help you out.

Roasted tuna

with five purées

4 x 75g tuna steaks, fully trimmed of skin and black meat

for the purées
225g unsalted butter
225g parsnips, peeled and finely chopped
225g carrots, peeled and finely chopped
225g beetroot, cooked and finely chopped
olive oil
225g frozen peas
570ml double cream
225g flat mushrooms
1 medium onion, finely chopped
150ml Madeira
570ml brown meat stock (veal or beef)
salt and white pepper

other ingredients
4 cherry tomatoes, grilled
4 fresh basil leaves, deep-fried
olive oil
juice of 1 lemon

For the parsnip purée: melt half of the butter, add the parsnips and sweat them off gently until soft – do not allow them to colour. Add enough water to cover the parsnips, reduce rapidly by a third, and season with salt and pepper. Blend in a food processor and add 150ml double cream. Adjust the seasoning and keep warm.

For the carrot purée: as above, but replace the parsnips with carrots.

For the beetroot purée: blend the beetroot, 1tbsp olive oil, salt and pepper in a food processor until smooth and pass through a fine sieve. Warm gently in a pan.

For the pea purée: place the peas in a pan, pour in enough water to cover them and boil for 2 minutes. Drain them and reserve the cooking liquor. Blend the peas in a food processor, and add half the cooking liquor and 120ml cream. Pass the purée through a fine sieve, season and keep warm.

For the mushroom purée: blend the mushrooms in a food processor. Sweat off the onion in 1tbsp olive oil – but do not allow it to colour. Add the mushrooms and sweat off the mixture again for a few moments. Turn up the heat, add the Madeira and reduce the mixture rapidly by half. Add the brown stock and reduce again by two-thirds. Blitz, then add 150ml cream, season and keep warm.

To serve, heat a little olive oil in a pan. Seal the tuna steaks until caramelised and golden brown in colour, but making sure they remain pink in the middle. Leave them to rest for 3 minutes. Using a spoon, make a line of each of the five purées across the plate. Place the tuna steaks in the middle and garnish with a grilled cherry tomato and a deep-fried basil leaf on top. Finish with a drizzle of olive oil and lemon juice.

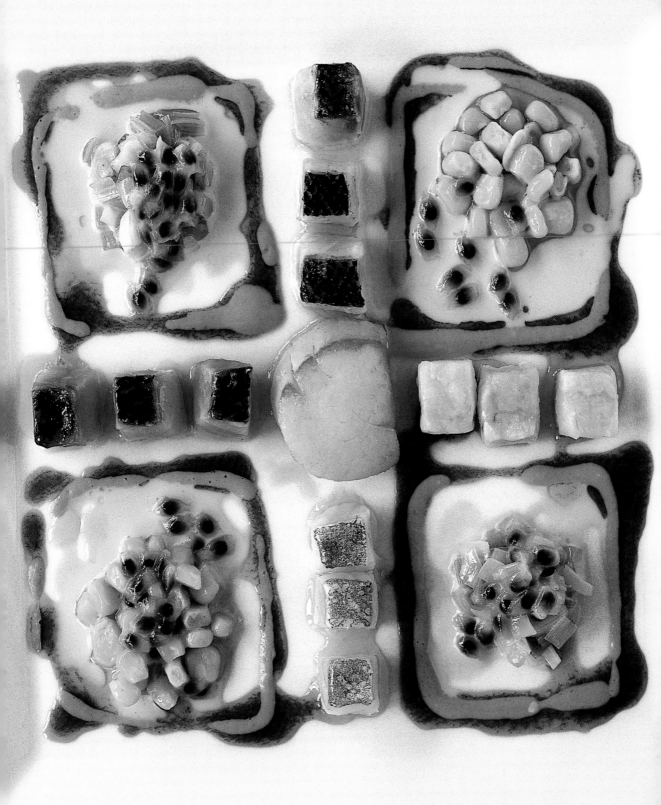

Assiette of fish

with passion fruit butter sauce and oyster vinaigrette

225g brill fillet
225g salmon fillet
110g cod tails
(All fish to be trimmed by
fishmonger – skin left on – and cut
into 1cm dice)
olive oil
4 scallops
a squeeze of lemon juice
1 leek, finely diced
kernels of 1 corn on the cob
salt and white pepper

for the vinaigrette
4 oysters
150ml olive oil
4 cherry tomatoes
1 red pepper, diced
55ml water
salt and white pepper

for the butter sauce
275ml fish stock
110g unsalted butter
1tbsp olive oil
salt and white pepper
seeds of 1 passion fruit

Preheat the oven to 230°C (gas mark 8). Place the fish pieces on a baking tray, coat them with olive oil and put them to one side.

For the vinaigrette: open the oysters, wash them thoroughly and blend them in a food processor with the olive oil, cherry tomatoes, red pepper, water and seasoning. Pass the vinaigrette through a fine sieve and refrigerate.

For the butter sauce: reduce the fish stock by two-thirds. Add the butter and whisk thoroughly. Season and add the olive oil. Blend in a food processor, pass through a fine sieve and keep warm.

Put the fish in the oven for 3–4 minutes until cooked. Pan-fry the scallops in a drop of olive oil until golden brown, and season with salt and lemon juice. Sauté the sweetcorn and leeks separately in 1tbsp olive oil. Add the passion fruit seeds to the butter sauce.

To serve, put the fish, scallops, sweetcorn and leeks on a plate, spoon the oyster vinaigrette around them, and finish with olive oil and the warm butter sauce.

Pan-fried saddle of rabbit

with crab bisque and chive dressing

2 whole rabbit saddles (including liver and kidney), taken off the bone by butcher

for the crab bisque
1 medium onion
1 medium carrot
2 celery stalks
1 leek
1 garlic bulb
2tbsp olive oil
meat of 1 crab
110g tomato purée
275ml red wine
275ml white wine
1.2 litre water
1 lemon, sliced
275ml double cream

for the dressing
1 pack of chives
275ml olive oil
salt and white pepper

other ingredients
12 quail eggs
olive oil
2 medium onions, finely sliced
450g carrots, diced (1cm) and cooked
unsalted butter
2 globe artichokes, peeled, cut into 4 and cooked
1 small pack chervil, in large sprigs
salt and black pepper

For the crab bisque: finely chop the vegetables and garlic, and sauté them in olive oil until golden brown. Add the crab meat and sweat it off for 5 minutes. Mix in the tomato purée and wine, add the water and chopped lemons, and cook on a low gas for 2 hours. Pass through a fine sieve, return to the pan and reduce by two-thirds. Add the cream and put the bisque to one side.

For the dressing: blitz the ingredients in a food processor, pass the mixture through a fine sieve and chill in the fridge until needed.

For the vegetables and egg: poach the quail eggs for 2 minutes, and season them with olive oil and salt. Fry the onions in 1tbsp olive oil until golden brown and crispy, and gently warm the cooked carrots in a knob of butter and season. Fry the cooked artichokes in 1tbsp olive oil until golden brown.

For the rabbit: preheat the oven to 180°C (gas mark 4). Fry the rabbit saddles in an ovenproof pan for 4 minutes so that they are still pink inside, then roast them in the oven for 2 minutes only before allowing them to rest for about 5 minutes. Then carve both of them into 8 long slices. Pan-fry the rabbit kidney and liver in a little olive oil until crisp but still pink inside.

To serve, gently warm the crab bisque in a frying pan, whisking it into a froth using a balloon whisk. Deep-fry the chervil and season it. Assemble the dish, and finish with the foamy sauce, the chive dressing and a drizzle of olive oil.

Watermelon soup

with frozen yoghurt mousse decorated with
chocolate seeds

for the stock syrup
110g caster sugar
275ml water

for the watermelon soup
5 cups red watermelon, blitzed
and passed through a fine seive
juice of 1 lemon

for the mousse
150g caster sugar
50ml water
3 egg whites
150ml double cream
250g plain yoghurt

for the garnish
25g dark chocolate
honeydew melon, finely diced

For the stock syrup: bring the water and sugar to the boil, simmer for 3 minutes, remove from the heat and allow to cool.

For the watermelon soup: blend the watermelon, lemon juice and stock syrup and refrigerate until required.

For the mousse: boil the water and half of the sugar to soft ball stage (230°C). Slowly whip the egg whites into soft peaks with an electric mixer on medium speed. Turn the mixer on high and slowly pour the sugar mixture down the side of the bowl, whipping it until it is cool to touch. Whisk together the cream and remaining sugar. Then fold in the egg-white mixture and yoghurt, pour it into four greased 2.5cm ring moulds and freeze.

For the chocolate seeds: place small dots of melted chocolate, the size of watermelon seeds, on chilled baking paper. Using the tip of a knife, make a small tail to the base of the dots. Refrigerate until ready to use.

To serve, pour the watermelon soup into individual bowls. Remove the mousse from the rings by running a hot knife around the inside, then top each one with finely diced honeydew melon and place in the centre of each bowl. Place several chocolate seeds around the soup to create a watermelon effect.

Ian Morgan
Rhodes & Co

Ian Morgan
Rhodes & Co

I have always enjoyed cooking, especially baking with my mother when I was growing up. And, in a sense, one of the best things for me about being Head Chef at Rhodes & Co is being able to bring together a young team of cooks and watch them grow together and develop their skills.

After a traditional Trust House Forte apprenticeship lasting six years, I worked as Sous Chef at The Randolph Hotel in Oxford, Head Chef at The Bear Hotel in Woodstock and then as Sous Chef at The Lanesborough's Conservatory, before joining the Rhodes team in 1999 to open up a new establishment opposite Old Trafford. The restaurant we created offers Rhodes classics alongside many other new and exciting dishes, but all of our food is united by four simple tenets: high quality, honest flavour, good texture and value for money.

The match-day breakfasts here are absolutely frantic and I love Saturday nights when the atmosphere can be quite electric. So, if I could manage both this and one or two more of Rhodes' expanding establishments, I'd be very happy.

Grilled sardine fillets on crostini

with a sauce remoulade

4 thick slices of 'uncut' white, brown, granary or flavoured (e.g. onion) bread
olive oil and unsalted butter for brushing
8 fresh sardines, scaled and filleted (16 fillets)
4 shallots, cut into 2mm rings
milk and plain flour to coat
paprika
2tbsp good olive oil
2tbsp red wine vinegar
sea salt and milled white pepper
green salad leaves

for the sauce remoulade

100ml mayonnaise, readymade
1tsp gherkin, finely chopped
1tsp capers, finely chopped
1tsp Dijon mustard
1 heaped tsp mixed fresh herbs (e.g. parsley, tarragon and chervil), chopped
1 small anchovy fillet, finely chopped
squeeze of lemon juice
coarse sea salt and white pepper

For the sauce remoulade: add all the ingredients to the mayonnaise, seasoning with sea salt and pepper.

For the crostini: liberally brush the bread with olive oil, and toast until golden. Once at room temperature, spread each slice generously with the sauce remoulade.

For the sardines: place the fillets – 4 per portion – top-to-tail on a greased baking tray and brush well with butter to protect the flesh and help the skin to crisp. Season with sea salt and a twist of pepper before placing under a preheated hot grill for about 4–5 minutes – even less dependant on size – to cook and crisp up.

Meanwhile, add a touch of paprika to the flour. Pass the shallot rings carefully through the milk, drain them, then pass them through the flour. Shake off any excess and fry for 2–3 minutes until golden. Mix together the oil, vinegar and seasoning to make a dressing.

To serve, dress the salad leaves with the dressing, and arrange them neatly over the crostini. Lay the cooked fillets across the top, transfer to a plate, and carefully arrange the shallot rings over them. Spoon any remaining dressing neatly around the edge.

Prawn, tomato and pea linguini

450g lobster shells/675g lobster
1.2–1.5 litre fish stock
225–350g linguini noodles
225–300g prawns, peeled and
cooked
175g fresh peas, blanched
4 plum tomatoes, blanched,
peeled, de-seeded and diced
salt and white pepper
for the sauce
25g unsalted butter
1tbsp olive oil
1 large carrot, roughly diced
2–3 shallots or 1 large onion,
roughly diced
2 celery sticks, roughly diced
1 small leek, roughly diced
1 fennel bulb, roughly diced
1 garlic clove, crushed
1 star anise (optional)
strip of orange zest
fresh basil leaves, bruised
fresh tarragon leaves, bruised
a pinch of saffron, soaked
50ml brandy
8 large ripe tomatoes, quartered
1tsp tomato purée
salt and white pepper
a pinch of cayenne pepper
375ml dry white wine
150ml single cream (optional)
a few drops of lemon juice
for the dressing
150ml olive oil
juice of 1 lemon
zest of ½ lemon
1 cube brown rock sugar
50g prawn shells
3–4 white peppercorns

For the lobster: if using lobster shells, bring the fish stock to the boil, drop in the shells and simmer for 15 minutes. If using a live lobster, bring the fish stock to the boil and drop in the lobster. Cook for 3–4 minutes, remove the pan from the heat and leave the lobster in the stock for about 12 minutes until completely cooked. This will help flavour the stock and keep the lobster meat moist. Then break off the claws and crack them open with the back of a heavy knife to release the meat. The joint connecting the claw to the body should also be cracked open and the meat removed. Split the body and tail through the middle lengthways and remove the tail meat. Place the lobster meat in a little of the cooking liquor to keep it moist. It can be used as a garnish for this dish or in another recipe.

Reserve the lobster stock, and put the shells – whether from the live lobster, or bought separately – in a saucepan and crush them up as finely as possible with a rolling pin.

For the sauce: melt the butter with the olive oil in a large pan. Add the diced carrot, shallots or onion, celery, leek and fennel, along with the crushed garlic, star anise, orange zest, basil and tarragon leaves. Add the pinch of saffron and cook on a medium heat for 10–15 minutes so that the vegetables begin to soften but do not colour.

Add the crushed lobster shells and cook for a further 10 minutes. Add the brandy and, if possible, flambé the contents of the pan. Boil the mixture until almost dry, then add lobster stock, the quartered tomatoes and tomato purée and continue to simmer for 25–30 minutes. Blitz the sauce, with the shells and vegetables included, to a smooth consistency and strain it through a fine sieve to remove any shell, but pushing all of the flavour through. If the sauce is too thick, adjust the consistency with a little extra fish stock, and season with salt, white pepper and a pinch of cayenne pepper. The sauce is now ready to use but, for a creamier finish, add the single cream – a splash at a time – to taste. To lift the whole flavour, add a drop or two of lemon juice.

For the linguini: blanch the pasta in boiling salted water and, when tender to the bite, remove it from the heat and drain. Drop in the prawns and peas, and warm the mixture in a little of the sauce. Season, and mix in the tomatoes.

To serve, spoon a generous portion of the pasta on to a dish, frothing up the remaining sauce with a hand blender and spooning it over the pasta. Combine the dressing ingredients together and drizzle it around the edge to finish.

Ian Morgan
Rhodes & Co

Duck and black pudding sausages

with spring greens and pickled red onions

for the onions

450g red onions
95–120ml olive oil
95–120ml groundnut oil
95–120ml balsamic vinegar
a squeeze of fresh lemon juice
salt and black pepper

for the sausages

225g duck meat
110g pork meat, preferably leg or
shoulder, trimmed
55g pork back fat
110g black pudding
1 large onions, finely chopped
5g unsalted butter
½tsp ground mace
1 clove of garlic, crushed
(optional)
1 medium slice white bread,
crusts removed, made into
breadcrumbs
½ egg, beaten
a dash of Worcestershire sauce
salt and white pepper
about 1m fresh sausage casing,
thoroughly washed
olive oil and a knob of butter for
frying (optional)

for the spring greens

3–4 spring greens or 1 small
savoy cabbage, shredded
25g unsalted butter
salt and white pepper

For the pickled red onions: the pickled red onions can be made well in advance – at least 1–2 hours before serving. Cut the onions into 6 or 8, making sure that the core or root is still intact as this holds them together. Bring a pan of water to the boil, add the onions and cook for 1–2 minutes. Meanwhile, gently warm together the oils, vinegar and lemon juice. When ready, drain off the onions and, whilst still warm, coat them with the oil mixture, season immediately, and leave to marinate, turning them every now and again. They should be served at room temperature rather than hot so that the flavours do not get lost.

For the sausages: for the best results, place the mincing attachment in the fridge an hour before you start cooking. Mince the meats and black pudding to a medium-coarse texture – for a finer finish, mince through twice – and chill them in the fridge for a couple of hours. Sweat the onions in the butter until soft and add the mace and garlic (optional). Allow the mixture to cool, stir it into the meats, season, then add the breadcrumbs, egg and a drop of Worcestershire sauce.

Make a small amount of the sausage mixture into a little 'burger' the size of a 10p piece. Fry it off in a little olive oil for about 3 minutes on each side, and then break it in half. If the meat is still pink, continue cooking. When the meat is cooked through, taste it and adjust the seasoning and mace content in the rest of the sausage mixture accordingly. Cut the sausage casing into 12cm lengths and knot these at one end. Then, using a 1cm piping tube, gather the casing up on to the tube and pipe the mixture in until it is only half full. Any excess skin will tighten to create a perfect sausage-shape during cooking rather than becoming too taut. Seal each sausage with a knot at the other end too and keep them in the fridge until ready.

For the spring greens: blanch the spring greens in salted water for 2–3 minutes until tender, then toss them in butter and seasoning.

To prepare the dish, pan-fry or grill the sausages for 6–7 minutes on each side until golden brown and the juices run clear. Place some marinated onions on the plate, with the spring greens on top followed by the sausages, and drizzle any left-over onion marinade around the edge as a dressing.

Profiteroles

with hot chocolate sauce

for the choux pastry

150ml water

100g unsalted butter

pinch of salt

1 level tsp caster sugar

150g plain flour

3 medium eggs, beaten

for the pastry cream

2 egg yolks

40g caster sugar

12g cornflour

150ml milk

2 vanilla pods, split with the seeds removed

20ml double cream

15g unsalted butter

for the chocolate sauce

150g bitter dark chocolate, chopped

75g unsalted butter

40–50ml double cream

For the choux pastry: preheat the oven to 220°C (gas mark 7). Bring the water up to the boil, along with the butter, sugar and salt, and cook for 1 minute. Remove from the heat and beat in the flour to form a paste. Once smooth, return the pan to the heat and stir for 1½–2 minutes. Put the dough into a bowl, allow it to cool, then add the eggs one at a time, mixing thoroughly until smooth. Pipe approximately 25mm-wide, pea-shaped balls on to a lightly greased baking tray and bake in the oven until golden brown – about 10–15 minutes depending on size. Leave the door open for the last 2 minutes of cooking time, remove them from the heat and leave to cool on a cooling rack.

For the pastry cream: place the yolks, sugar and cornflour in a bowl and whisk until well blended. Bring the milk and vanilla pods to the boil, and whisk them into the egg mixture, then transfer everything back into the pan. Stir the mixture constantly for 3–5 minutes over a medium heat until it thickens, remove it from the heat and stir in the cream and butter. Allow the mixture to cool and knock it back.

For the chocolate sauce: place all the ingredients together in a bowl over simmering water until the chocolate has completely melted, stirring well. This sauce is best served warm.

To serve, slice each profiterole in half and pipe a generous portion of the pastry cream into each side. Sandwich them back together again, and pour over the warm sauce, dusting with icing sugar to finish.

Jem O'Sullivan
The Lincoln

Jem O'Sullivan
The Lincoln

I was always a bit of a skiver at school, but things changed when I was given a four-week placement at The Steak and Kebab House in Didsbury. In a sense, that sealed my fate because from that point onwards I knew that I wanted to become a chef. On finishing school, I got my City and Guilds and was lucky enough to land a job at The Lime Tree, working and learning under its owner and Head Chef, Patrick Hannity. Less than a year later, he made me Head Chef at his second restaurant, Primavera, where I stayed for three years before moving back to The Lime Tree again. After four more years as Head Chef there, I was poached by Fred Dome to open up his new venture, The Lincoln. And open it up I really did. I was there literally from day one, as the building was gradually transformed from dowdy ex-DSS premises into the fresh, contemporary-looking restaurant it is today.

The Lincoln opened in September 1998 and the dishes chosen here reflect our unique style of modern British fusion cooking. My influences come from eating in other people's restaurants and from holidays abroad, and this combination seems to have struck the right chord. We won three major awards in our first year – Chef of the Year, Restaurant of the Year and an AA rosette – and now we all work hard to maintain these high standards consistently across every dish. We have had a couple of bad experiences, like when one of our commis chefs managed to set fire to an oven at 5.55 p.m. on a Friday night – not the best time to have to start all the prep again. But overall I am proud of the easy-going ambience of the kitchen, and I am eternally grateful to all my staff for maintaining the quality of our food and presentation, because this makes me look good too!

Chilli rubbed carpaccio of tuna

with wasabi dressing, avocado salsa and herb salad

allow 110g tuna per person (ask for blue fin tuna middle loin)

for the tuna rub

2tbsp chilli flakes, crushed
1tbsp fennel seeds
2tbsp cumin seeds
2tbsp mixed pepper, coarsely ground
4tbsp fresh coriander, chopped
1 tbsp olive oil

for the avocado salsa

3 large avocados, slightly over-ripe
1 red pepper, finely diced
1 carrot, finely diced
1 red onion, finely diced
4 large tbsp crème fraiche
salt and black pepper

for the wasabi dressing

1 tube of prepared wasabi
2tbsp water
275ml vegetable oil
juice of ½ a lime
juice of 1 lemon
salt and black pepper

for the herb salad

2 frizzy lettuce heads, torn
1tbsp fresh chives
1tbsp fresh chervil
1tbsp fresh mint
1tbsp fresh coriander

For the tuna rub: it's best to prepare the tuna at least one day in advance if you can. Take all the dry ingredients, gently roast them in a dry pan until the spices give off an aroma, allow them to cool, then spread them on to a flat tray. Take the tuna loin and roll it in the spices until it is covered all over, before coating it with coriander in the same way. Next wrap the tuna in cling film, roll it into a sausage shape and leave it in the fridge over-night. Then take the tuna out of the cling film and sear it off by rolling it around in a little olive oil for 35–40 seconds until it is golden brown. Wrap it up in the cling film as before and leave it to cool once more.

For the avocado salsa: skin the avocados, remove the seeds and dice them as finely as possible, like the vegetables. Place them all into a mixing bowl and stir in the crème fraiche, seasoning to taste.

For the wasabi dressing: place the wasabi paste in a bowl and add the water. Slowly add the oil a little at a time, and finish with the lime and lemon juice, seasoning to taste.

Once the dressing is made, take the tuna from the fridge and slice it as thinly as possible, allowing 3–4 slices per person. Place these completely flat on the plate. Next put a good spoonful of the avocado salsa in the middle of the tuna, then take the herbs and lettuce and mix them with a touch of wasabi dressing, putting a small amount of them on top of the salsa. To finish, put a small drizzle of wasabi dressing around the plate. Alternatively, serve this dish with scallops and deep-fried sweet potato as shown in the photograph.

Thai monkish

with sweet potato mash and crab spring rolls

150–200g monkfish per person
(request it off the bone and
skinned)

for the Thai marinade

6 red chillies
6 lemon-grass stalks
2tbsp fresh ginger, chopped
2 bunches of fresh coriander
4 cloves of garlic
juice of 2 limes

for the sweet potato mash

800g sweet potatoes, peeled and
chopped
1.70 litres milk
salt and black pepper
1tbsp Thai marinade
a dash of coconut milk

for the coconut dressing

400ml tin of coconut milk, chilled
1tbsp Thai marinade (or Thai
paste)
2tbsp fresh coriander, chopped

for the spring rolls

300g fresh crab meat
1tbsp fresh coriander, chopped
juice of 1 lemon
salt and black pepper
1 packet of spring roll pastry
1 egg, beaten
vegetable oil

For the Thai marinade: put all the ingredients into a blender and blitz them until they form a paste. Reserve 2tbsp for the potato mash and coconut dressing, and cover the monkfish with the rest, leaving it to marinate for 8–10 hours.

For the spring roll: mix the crab meat, coriander, lemon juice and seasoning together and keep them in the fridge for 1 hour. Then make diamond shapes with the pastry, put a tablespoon of the mixture in the bottom corner, and roll the pastry up tightly halfway towards the top. Brush the beaten egg on all the remaining edges, fold the sides inwards and continue rolling the mixture up to the top.

For the sweet potato mash: cover the chopped potato with the milk in a pan, season to taste and simmer gently until tender. Drain off the milk, add the coconut oil and 1tbsp of the reserved Thai marinade and mash the potato until smooth, keeping it warm on one side until needed.

For the coconut dressing: the coconut milk will separate if kept in the fridge, so pour off the solid cream into a pan and warm it through gently. Then add the remaining Thai marinade and coriander and allow them to infuse in the milk for 2 minutes, taking care that it does not boil.

To prepare the dish, preheat the oven to 200°C (gas mark 6). Seal the marinated monkfish on all sides in an ovenproof pan, then place it in the oven for 5–6 minutes. Meanwhile, deep-fry the spring rolls in vegetable oil for 3 minutes or until golden brown. When cooked, place the monkfish on a plate along with the warm sweet potato mash, spring roll and warm dressing and serve.

Jem O'Sullivan
The Lincoln

Pan-fried fillet steak

with smoked bacon and crushed potato cake,

wilted spinach and Cornish pasty

allow 175–200g beef fillet per person
salt and black pepper
3 bags baby spinach leaves
25g unsalted butter

for the potato cake

900g new potatoes
450g smoked bacon back, grilled and thinly sliced
4tbsp fresh parsley, chopped
4tbsp fresh chives, chopped
50g plain flour
6 eggs, beaten
breadcrumbs for dusting
olive oil for deep-frying
salt and black pepper

for the Cornish pasty

400g plain flour
225g unsalted butter
4tbsp water
1 small onion, finely chopped
1 celery stick, finely chopped
2 small carrots, finely chopped
1tbsp fresh thyme, chopped
450g minced beef
salt and black pepper
1 stock cube
1 egg, beaten

For the potato cake: cook the potatoes in boiling salted water until soft, drain and leave on one side. Once cool, crush them with your hands to a rough consistency and mix in the bacon, parsley and chives. Mould the mixture into small cake shapes (about 6–7cm in diameter) and cover them in flour, then in egg, then in flour again and finally in breadcrumbs. Leave on one side.

For the Cornish pasty: rub together the sifted flour, a pinch of salt and 200g butter until it resembles breadcrumbs. Add enough water to form a soft dough, wrap it in cling film and leave it in the fridge. Then melt the remaining butter in a pan and cook down the onion, celery and carrot for 1–1½ minutes until softened. Add the thyme and mince and fry this for 5–10 minutes until completely cooked. Then crumble in the stock cube and put the mixture in the fridge.

When the mixture is cool, preheat the oven to 180°C (gas mark 4). Roll out the pastry to ½cm thick and cut it into 10cm disks. Put a small amount of the mince in the middle of each disk and brush the outer edge with egg. Then bring the edges up to the centre, stick them together to form a semi-circle and pinch the edges with your fingertips to give the appearance of a Cornish pasty. Bake in the oven for about 8 minutes until golden brown.

To prepare the dish, season the fillet on both sides and pan-fry it in a little olive oil to your preferred level (well-done, medium or rare). Deep-fry the potato cakes for about 2½ minutes, until golden brown, and wilt down the spinach for 30–40 seconds in a little butter, placing it on the plate. Position the potato cake on top, followed by the fillet and serve topped with the Cornish pasty.

Jem O'Sullivan
The Lincoln

Chocolate truffle cake

with raspberry coulis

for the truffle
450g good dark chocolate
570ml double cream
4 egg yolks
50g caster sugar

for the topping
110g dark chocolate
65ml double cream
25g unsalted butter

for the coulis
4 punnets of raspberries
200g caster sugar

For the truffle: break up the chocolate and place it, along with half of the cream, into a bowl inside a pan of water. Then melt the chocolate and cream together over a gentle heat. Whisk the egg yolks with the sugar until pale and fluffy. Semi-whip the rest of the cream, add the egg mixture, then fold in the melted chocolate mixture. Spoon the truffle to the desired thickness on to a greased baking tray and chill in the fridge while you prepare the topping.

For the topping: melt the chocolate and all the cream as before, then add the butter.

For the coulis: place the raspberries and sugar in a pan. Heat them over a low heat until they have cooked down, and pass them through a fine sieve.

To serve, use a knife to spread a layer of topping over the chilled truffle mixture. Then glaze it, either under the grill or using a blow-torch, before cutting it into the desired shape, and carefully spooning the coulis around the edge.

Steven Saunders
The Lowry

Steven Saunders
The Lowry

Like many chefs, I have always had a love of food and have been cooking since I was a young boy. I trained at the Savoy Hotel in London, and I must admit that my first ever job – at the Marlborough Hotel in my home town of Ipswich – now seems a million miles away from the journalism and TV programmes like *Ready, Steady Cook* for which most people know me today. It was still an important grounding, though, helping me along the way towards becoming Young Restaurateur of the Year in 1991, with the National Restaurant of the Year award following in 1995 for The Pink Geranium.

My food is colourful, fresh and honest. I am passionate about making the most of British seasonal produce and, as you will see in my recipes, I use organic ingredients wherever possible. Indeed, my ambition is to open a whole fleet of organic restaurants throughout the UK, and this dream is beginning to come true – the first one, Organica, is launching in London soon.

In a sense The Lowry needs no introduction. It was the country's second millennium project – a sensational flagship centre for the arts that was justifiably awarded Building of the Year 2001. The Lowry restaurant commands an enviable position within the complex, complementing the theatres, galleries and cafés, and I feel privileged to have been involved in setting up this exciting project from the start. Indeed, so successful have we been that the restaurant was voted 'Best Newcomer of the Year' in the Hi Life Diners Club Restaurant of the Year Awards 2001.

The dishes I have selected for this book represent a good cross section of the style of British food we serve: some classic, some modern and a proportion leaning towards the East.

Spicy sweetcorn soup

with roasted lobster and a shellfish oil garnish

Serves 6

575g whole live lobster
1 slice of lemon (optional)
1tsp unsalted butter
for the shellfish oil garnish
1tbsp light olive oil
1 medium onion or 2 shallots,
finely sliced
2 cloves of garlic, crushed
2 sticks of celery, chopped
1 leek, chopped
2tbsp cold-pressed organic virgin
olive oil
a squeeze of lemon juice
salt and white pepper
for the sweetcorn soup
1 medium onion, finely chopped
2 cloves of garlic, finely chopped
1 red chilli, thinly sliced
1 leek, finely chopped
1tsp olive oil
2tsp turmeric, ground, or ½tsp
saffron threads
1 bag frozen organic sweetcorn
kernels (approx. 900g)
1 litre lobster stock (or organic
fish or vegetable stock)
salt and white pepper
2tbsp double cream or crème
fraiche to finish

For the lobster: bring a large pan of salted water to the boil, adding a slice of lemon to help the flavour if you wish. Drop in the live lobster, allow the water to come back to the boil and cook it for 5–7 minutes until it is red in colour. Remove the lobster immediately and cool it in iced water. Cut off the tail and cut it in half lengthways through the shell. Then cut each half into half again the other way so that you have 4 quarters, and leave them in the fridge, along with the left-over shell, until needed.

For the shellfish oil garnish: nowadays you can obtain some very good liquid fish and lobster stocks, but although these will save you time, I'm afraid they won't be as good! Preheat the oven to 230°C (gas mark 8). Roast the lobster shell in a little light olive oil for 30–40 minutes until it is crisp and fragile but not blackened. Add the onion, garlic, celery and leek, pour in enough cold water just to cover everything, and simmer for 2–3 hours on the stove. Strain the stock through a fine sieve and reserve the liquor. To make the shellfish oil, simply reduce about 2tbsp of the liquor until you have about 1tbsp of concentrated stock. Add about twice this amount of the olive oil and a squeeze of lemon juice, whisk and season to taste.

For the sweetcorn soup: sauté the onion, garlic, chilli and leek in the olive oil for about 5 minutes in a medium saucepan until translucent. Then add the turmeric and sweetcorn and stir well. Pour in the stock and bring this to the boil, before reducing the heat and simmering for 30 minutes. Blend it well in a food processor and return it to a clean pan. Taste, season well and add the cream to emulsify the soup.

To prepare the dish, either grill the lobster tail quarters or place them in a hot oven with a teaspoon of unsalted butter on top and season well. Cook them for 5 minutes, then serve on top of the soup with a drizzle of shellfish oil.

Roasted monkfish

with a coriander and macadamia nut crust
and lemon-grass liquor

4 x175–200g pieces of monkfish
cut through the bone
salt and white pepper
light olive oil

for the crust
60g unsalted butter
2tbsp macadamia nuts
1tbsp fresh coriander
juice of 1 lemon
1tbsp olive oil
salt and white pepper

for the sauce
I medium onion, thinly sliced
1 clove of garlic, crushed and
roughly chopped
3 sticks of lemon grass, bruised
with the back of a knife and
chopped into 4
2 green chillies, thinly sliced
1 leek, finely sliced
1tbsp light olive oil
approx. 450g fish bones (monkfish
or any white fish)
2 x 400g tins organic coconut milk
2–3 Kaffir leaves (optional)
4tbsp double cream to finish
salt and white pepper
fresh lemon juice (optional)

for the pak choy (or bok choy)
1tbsp light olive oil or grapeseed
oil
½tbsp galangal Thai ginger or
root ginger, chopped
1 clove of garlic, chopped
2 small pak choy
salt and white pepper
truffle oil to finish (optional)

For the crust: blend the ingredients in a food processor, taste, season well and reserve.

For the sauce: sweat the onion, garlic, lemon grass, chilli and leek in a little light olive oil until soft. Add the fish bones, stir them in well, then add the coconut milk and Kaffir leaves. Bring the sauce to the boil, simmer it for 30 minutes and then pass it through a fine sieve into a clean saucepan. Add the double cream to help emulsify the sauce and season well. (You may need a little fresh lemon juice to sharpen the flavours.)

For the monkfish: cooking the monkfish on the bone will give it a lovely, sweet and juicy flavour and help to keep the fish moist. But don't be afraid of the bone. It's unlike other fish bones since it is actually in one large piece. Preheat the oven to 180°C (gas mark 4) and line an ovenproof frying pan with a butter wrapper or greaseproof paper. Season the fish well and seal it in the pan on all sides in a little oil. Then put the pan in the oven and roast the fish pieces through for 7–10 minutes until the juice runs white and comes to the surface. At this point, the fish should be fairly soft, so remove it and allow it to rest briefly for 1 minute. Then spread the crust thinly on the top of each piece and return them to the oven or grill to brown for 2–4 minutes.

For the pak choy: heat up the olive oil in a wok and stir-fry the ginger and garlic for about 30 seconds until tender and lightly browned. Add the pak choy leaves whole, season well and fry for 30 seconds.

To serve, place the pak choy on a dish with the monkfish on top. Whizz up the sauce with a hand blender until frothy, and carefully spoon this around the edge, drizzling the fish with the truffle oil to finish.

Peppered free range Cheshire lamb

with swede fondant, baby spinach, garlic confit and reduced lamb jus

4 x175g loins of lamb, well trimmed
1 level tbsp cracked pepper, freshly milled
a little olive oil

for the lamb jus
approx. 1.8kg lamb bones (or 500ml organic lamb stock)
1tbsp olive oil (optional)
1 large onion, chopped
1 carrot, peeled and chopped
2 stalks celery, chopped
3 cloves of garlic, sliced in half lengthways
1 large bunch of fresh thyme (or 2tbsp), chopped
water, enough to cover bones
250ml red wine

for the swede fondant
2 medium swedes, peeled and cut into 4 x 8cm rounds
approx. 1 litre chicken stock
1 sprig of rosemary
60g unsalted butter

for the spinach
200g bag of baby spinach
25g unsalted butter
salt and black pepper
1 tsp ground nutmeg

for the garlic confit
4 cloves of garlic, unpeeled (preferably fresh wet garlic)
approx. 100ml olive oil, to cover garlic

other ingredients
18 small shallots, peeled and blanched until tender
a pinch of soft brown sugar
4 sprigs of thyme

For the lamb: drizzle a little olive oil over the lamb pieces, sprinkle them with the crushed pepper and, if preparing the dish in advance, roll them each tightly in cling film to draw the flavours into the meat. Keep them cool in the fridge until required.

For the lamb jus: preheat the oven to 200°C (gas mark 6). Roast off the lamb bones either in a little oil or as they are for about 45 minutes until golden brown. Place them in a deep saucepan with the vegetables, garlic and thyme, and cover with cold water. Bring the mixture to the boil, skim off any residue and simmer for about 4 hours. Strain the stock, add the red wine, and reduce until it has the consistency of whipping cream and coats the back of a spoon. You will need at least 2tbsp of well-reduced stock for this recipe. Finish with 1tbsp fresh thyme leaves, and sieve before serving.

For the fondant: preheat the oven to 180°C (gas mark 4). Place the swede rounds on a baking tray, cover them with the chicken stock, rosemary and butter, and bake them in the oven for about 20 minutes until tender.

For the garlic confit: place the garlic pieces in a small pan, cover them with oil and poach them gently for about 10 minutes until tender. Then remove the garlic and reserve the garlic-flavoured oil. Prepare, wash and pick the spinach.

Preheat the oven to 200°C (gas mark 6). Unwrap the lamb and sear it in a hot frying pan in a little light olive oil until sealed all over. Then roast it in an ovenproof frying pan lined with parchment paper in the oven for about 5–7 minutes, remove it from the heat and allow it to rest for 1 minute. Melt the butter in a wok, stir-fry the spinach for a few seconds, season it well and add the nutmeg. Then fry off the pre-blanched shallots in a little oil, adding a pinch of sugar to help colour them, and deep-fry the thyme sprigs in either your garlic oil or vegetable oil for about 10 seconds.

To serve, place the swede fondant in the centre of the plate. Carve the lamb into 6 slices, and arrange alternate layers of lamb and spinach so that you create a tower effect. Place the garlic confit on top and the glazed shallots – 3 per portion – around the dish. Drizzle the lamb jus around the plate, and garnish with the deep-fried thyme. Serve immediately. Alternatively, you could drizzle a little truffle oil around to cut the jus and add more depth of flavour, but don't serve the truffle oil in more than one course!

Rhubarb soufflé

with chilled sweet rhubarb lemonadade

300g caster sugar
1tbsp cold water
6 sticks fresh rhubarb, chopped
1 heaped tsp cornflour mixed with
1tsp cold water
18 egg whites
4tbsp granulated sugar
juice of 2 organic lemons

Butter and sugar four small 8cm ramekin dishes, preheat the oven to 200°C (gas mark 6), and chill or freeze 4 small glasses.

Put the caster sugar, water and chopped rhubarb in a pan, bring them to the boil and simmer for 10–15 minutes until soft. Strain off the rhubarb mixture and reserve the rhubarb juices. Take a third of these juices and add the cornflour mixture to thicken them.

Then whisk the egg whites until stiff and slowly whisk in the granulated sugar for about 30 seconds. Fold the whites into two-thirds of the cooked rhubarb mixture, and add the thickened rhubarb juices. Put the remaining rhubarb into the bottom of each ramekin dish, and spoon the egg white mixture on to the top – above the height of the ramekin so that it is already raised before they enter the oven. Place in the oven, and cook for 10 minutes until golden brown.

For the lemonade: add the lemon juice to the remaining rhubarb juices and pass this through a fine sieve before chilling.

Serve the hot soufflés immediately, with a glass of rhubarb lemonade on one side.

Kazuo Sonoda, Nick Jeffrey
and David Fox
Tampopo

Kazuo Sonoda, Nick Jeffrey and David Fox
Tampopo

It was the freshness and variety of the local cuisine in East Asia that got us thinking. Nick and I had both travelled extensively out there and it was the food bought from street hawker stalls that convinced us that there would be a demand for this style of Eastern food-on-the-go in the UK. And Manchester, with its vibrancy and cultural diversity, seemed the perfect location.

Along the way we had met and become friends with Kazuo Sonoda from Japan. He had recently moved to Manchester but, as he freely admits, English wasn't his strong point. So, armed with his knowledge of Eastern cooking and mystical ability with the wok, he started out as one of Tampopo's chefs. Now – four years and a language course later – he heads up the bustling, energetic kitchen, his Japanese inner calm and cheerful smile making him a natural leader.

The Tampopo team works very hard with both local and not-so-local suppliers to make sure that we get exactly the right ingredients to prepare almost all dishes and base sauces in-house from scratch. Our challenge is to make the food as authentic as possible, stretching the taste buds to new levels, whilst keeping the dishes accessible. Our greatest pleasure? Seeing a new customer walk out with a glazed look of delight on their face – just as we have both done on numerous occasions when experiencing new flavours on our travels. The following recipes represent all that is good about Tampopo – an Eastern odyssey across your taste buds.

Kazuo Sonoda, Nick Jeffrey and David Fox
Tampopo

Yakitori skewers

with a teriyaki sauce

for the teriyaki sauce
280ml water
70ml Mirin (Japanese cooking rice wine)
70ml Japanese light soy sauce
20ml sake (Japanese rice wine)
45gm caster sugar
1tsp potato starch
3tbsp cold water

for the skewers
600g chicken breast, skinned and boneless (approximately 3 chicken breasts)
6 spring onions
2tbsp vegetable oil
8 bamboo skewers

For the teriyaki sauce: place the water, Mirin, soy sauce, sake and sugar into a pan and heat them together until the sugar has dissolved. Pour half of the mixture into a separate pan – to baste the yakitori skewers during cooking – and bring the remainder to the boil. Then whisk the potato starch and water into a smooth paste and drizzle this into the lightly simmering teriyaki sauce. Stir continuously for 3 minutes and then keep warm on one side.

For the yakitori skewers: cut the chicken into 24 cubes. Cut the stems of each spring onion into four 2cm-long strips to give you 24 pieces. Then thinly slice the green tops of the spring onion for garnishing. Take 8 bamboo skewers and begin threading on pieces of chicken and spring onion, starting with the chicken and alternating this with the spring onion until you have 3 pieces of each on every skewer.

Heat the oil on a griddle or in a flat-bottom frying-pan. Place the yakitoris in the oil and fry them for 2 minutes on each side, basting three times with the unthickened teriyaki sauce that was set aside. Once cooked, place 2 skewers on each plate, drizzle with a little thickened teriyaki sauce and garnish with the thinly sliced spring onion to serve.

Mee goreng

spicy chicken noodles

for the sauce
2tbsp vegetable oil
15g red onion, finely chopped
1tsp garlic, finely chopped
1tsp fresh ginger, finely chopped
1tsp coriander root, finely
chopped
2tsp belecan (shrimp paste)
60ml ketsup manis (sweet soy
sauce)
60ml light soy sauce
25ml sambal oelek (Indonesian
chilli paste)
¼tsp ground turmeric

for the mee goreng
6tbsp vegetable oil
4 chicken breasts, sliced into
medium strips
2 tomatoes, quartered
1 medium white onion, thinly
sliced
1 red pepper, de-seeded and
thinly sliced
12 shiitake mushrooms, sliced
(button mushrooms will do)
375g packet of rice stick noodles,
3mm or 5mm thick, softened for 1
hour in cold water
12 bunches of choi sum leaves,
shredded
3 handfuls of bean sprouts
4 sprigs of coriander, coarsely
chopped

This is a spicy dish, so if you prefer a milder flavour, try the coconut prawns on p. 166.

For the sauce: heat the oil in a wok until it starts to smoke lightly, and fry off the red onion, garlic, ginger and coriander root for 15 seconds. Add the belecan, ketsup manis, soy sauce, sambal oelek and turmeric, and fry for a further minute. Set the sauce aside and allow to cool.

For the mee goreng: only two portions of this dish can fit into the wok at a time, so once you have served the first two plates, repeat the whole process with the remaining ingredients. (Use half of the listed ingredients each time.) The dish is cooked very quickly so you will not keep your guests waiting long. Heat 4tbsp oil in a wok until lightly smoking and fry off the chicken strips until golden brown. Set them aside and keep them warm. Then heat 2tbsp oil in a clean wok and fry off the tomato, onion, pepper and mushrooms for 2 minutes. Put the chicken strips back and stir-fry them again with the vegetables for 30 seconds before adding your sauce and stir-frying for a further 30 seconds. Add the soaked rice noodles, the shredded choi sum and a handful of beansprouts, and stir-fry for a final 2 minutes or until the noodles are soft and cooked. To serve, turn the mixture on to two dinner plates and garnish with beansprouts and coriander.

Kazuo Sonoda, Nick Jeffrey and David Fox
Tampopo

Prawns in coconut and basil sauce

4tbsp vegetable oil

1 medium white onion, thinly sliced

1 yellow pepper, thinly sliced

6 spring onions, thinly chopped

4 shallots, peeled and thinly sliced

500g tiger prawns (about 24), shelled and peeled

24 sweet Thai basil leaves and 4 tips for garnishing

4 cups long-grain rice, boiled

for the coconut sauce

1tbsp vegetable oil

10cm stalk of lemon grass, bashed and finely chopped

1tsp garlic, finely chopped

1tsp ginger, finely chopped

1tsp coriander root, finely chopped (the stems are better for lasting flavour)

6 lime leaves, finely chopped

400ml can coconut milk

250ml whipping cream

1tsp salt

1tsp ground white pepper

20g caster sugar

½tsp turmeric

This is a mild dish, so if you prefer more spice try the Mee goreng on p. 165 instead.

For the coconut sauce: heat the oil in a wok until lightly smoking and fry off the lemon grass, garlic, ginger, coriander root and lime leaves for 30 seconds. Add the coconut milk, cream, salt, pepper, sugar and turmeric and allow to simmer for 2 minutes. Set aside in another container and allow to cool.

To prepare the dish, heat the vegetable oil in a wok and stir-fry the onion, yellow pepper, spring onion and shallots until all are cooked and soft. Pour in the coconut sauce and bring to simmering point before turning down the heat to a light simmer. Add the tiger prawns and Thai basil leaves and allow to simmer for about 1 minute until the prawns are cooked. Serve on a bed of rice and garnish with the Thai basil tips.

Kazuo Sonoda, Nick Jeffrey and David Fox
Tampopo

Ginger crème brûlée

12 egg yolks
35g caster sugar
750ml whipping cream
½tsp vanilla essence
15g fresh ginger, finely chopped
mint leaves to garnish

Put 4 dessert bowls in the freezer for at least 20 minutes. Half-fill a large stainless steel bowl of iced water – in case the mixture splits during preparation. Beat together the egg yolks and caster sugar in a bowl. Place the cream, vanilla essence and chopped ginger into a pan and bring them almost to boiling point but without letting them actually boil. Then whisk the egg mixture while pouring in the heated cream, whisking all the time.

Rinse and dry the pan and pour the contents of the bowl back into it, cooking the mixture over a low heat until the custard thickens and you can see a trail left by the whisk – about 15–20 minutes. Stir constantly and be careful not to cook the egg yolks. If the mixture does look like it may split, submerge the bowl in the iced water to stop the cooking process. When the custard is thick, pour it into the frozen bowls and place in the fridge for 30 minutes to set.

When ready to serve, sprinkle the top of each with a little caster sugar and caramelise under a naked flame, garnishing with mint.

Harry Yeung
The Yang Sing

Harry Yeung
The Yang Sing

It was my father, a renowned chef from Hong Kong, who was among the first to introduce dim sum to this country when The Yang Sing opened in basement premises in George Street nearly 25 year ago. And, in a sense, I too have that same pioneering spirit. My great respect for tradition, combined with innovative ideas, meant that, right from the start, my cooking was cross-cultural – fusion cooking, as it is known today.

In a very real sense, therefore, our family business has always been at the forefront of culinary excellence, pushing forward the barriers whilst acting as the guardians of quality. I have an all-consuming passion for my art. For me, ingredients are everything and, despite the fact that I personally oversee all our three kitchens, I still go to the market every day to select fresh seasonal produce and visit Hong Kong regularly to choose the best from international suppliers.

This kind of attention to detail is one of the reasons we are recognised as Europe's leading Cantonese restaurant and I take great pride in the fact that, year after year, we continue to receive accolades and prestigious awards for our efforts. But it's not all been plain sailing. Watching our restaurant going up in smoke in 1997 was the worst experience of our lives, but the support of our loyal customers and the City of Manchester kept us going. Our triumph over adversity was captured by Granada TV in a five-part series entitled *The Yeung Ones* about the rebuilding of The Yang Sing.

The Yang Sing is undoubtedly a part of the city's fabric now and we all work hard to maintain that position. We have 200 à la carte dishes and there are always new and exciting creations to try – just talk to the staff.

Harry Yeung
The Yang Sing

Fruit and vegetable fried rice

25g pineapple pieces, chopped
25g apple pieces, peeled and
chopped
25g mange tout, chopped
25g raisins
1 ½tbsp vegetable oil
2 eggs, beaten
375g plain rice, boiled
½tsp salt
¼tsp Knorr chicken powder
25g iceberg lettuce, chopped

Blanche the pineapple and apple pieces, chopped mange tout and raisins in salted boiling water for 2 minutes. Heat up a wok to a high temperature, pour in the oil and grease the inside thoroughly. Add the beaten egg and fold it over until half-cooked, then add the boiled rice, stir-frying for about 1 ½ minutes. Add the seasoning and continue to stir-fry for another 1 ½ minutes, then stir in the blanched fruit, continuing to stir-fry for a further 1 ½ minutes. Finally, add the iceberg lettuce, and turn and mix it through evenly. The rice is ready to serve.

Harry Yeung
The Yang Sing

Black pepper and honey ostrich casserole

for the marinade

1 celery stick, chopped
1 small carrot, chopped
1 small stem lemon grass, chopped
2 or 3 sprigs of fresh coriander
250ml water
½tsp granulated sugar
½tsp salt
½tsp chicken stock powder
2tsp soy sauce
2tsp cornflour
2tsp dry white wine
potato starch (with water added)

for the casserole

450g ostrich fillet, sliced thinly into
5cm strips
vegetable oil
1 clove of garlic, chopped
½ large red pepper, diced (1cm)
½ large green pepper, diced (1cm)
1 leek, chopped into 2½cm lengths
1 spring onion, chopped into 2½cm
lengths
black pepper to taste

for the seasoning

½tsp black pepper powder
½tsp salt
½tsp chicken stock powder
a pinch of white pepper powder
a few drops of sesame oil
1tbsp oyster sauce
1tsp dark soy sauce
4tbsp chicken stock
potato starch (with water added)
1tsp rice wine
1tbsp clear honey

For the marinade: blend the celery, carrot and lemon grass with the coriander and water. Sieve the mixture into a large bowl, add the rest of the ingredients and stir several times with a wooden spoon. Then add the ostrich slices and marinade them for 1–2 hours.

For the casserole: bring a wok to a high temperature, pour in generous amounts of vegetable oil and bring it to a high temperature. Fry the ostrich strips in the hot oil for approximately 30 seconds, then drain off the oil. Clean the wok, bring it back to a high temperature again and add 1tbsp vegetable oil. Add the garlic and black pepper, followed by the green and red peppers, leek and spring onion, and stir-fry these for 30 seconds. Then add the fried ostrich and continue to stir-fry for another 30 seconds. Pour in the rice wine and chicken stock whilst still stir-frying and then add all the remaining seasoning, adding the honey last. Mix the potato starch with a little water to the required consistency and add this slowly whilst stir-frying to thicken. Serve in a hot casserole dish.

King prawn

with Sichuan sauce

450g king prawns, frozen
vegetable oil

for the sauce

1 clove of garlic, crushed
10g fresh ginger, finely chopped
25g onion, freshly chopped
½ red chilli, very finely chopped
10g coriander stem, finely
chopped
25g preserved turnip, finely
chopped
1tsp tomato sauce
½tsp hot bean paste
½tsp rice wine
½tsp salt
½tsp granulated sugar
½tsp potato starch
½tsp sweet Chinese vinegar*
a few drops of sesame oil
110g chicken stock

This dish has a sweet, hot and sour flavour with a special coriander taste. To produce it, however, the prawns must be completely covered by the sauce.

For the prawns: take off the shells, open the back of the prawns, and take out the vein. Make sure the prawns are thoroughly defrosted and washed. Blanch them in a pan of boiling water for 1 minute and then quickly deep-fry them in a wok in hot vegetable oil. Drain off the oil and keep the prawns on one side.

For the sauce: heat the wok again with a few drops of oil, then add the garlic, ginger, onion, chilli, coriander stem and preserved turnip and allow them to cook for half a minute. Add the tomato sauce and the hot bean paste, cook for a further 30 seconds, then add the prawns and the wine, chicken stock, salt and sugar, and cook for one minute. Thicken the dish with the potato starch, then add the vinegar and sesame oil and serve.

*NOTE: Chi Kiang Vi is a sweet Chinese vinegar and can be obtained from Chinese supermarkets. However, it is very expensive, and you can add sugar to an English malt vinegar in order to get the required taste.

Harry Yeung
The Yang Sing

Bunny-shaped dumplings

for the filling

700g prawns, frozen or fresh
½tsp salt
a pinch of white pepper
¼tsp chicken stock powder
a few drops of sesame oil
¼tsp granulated sugar
75g winter bamboo shoots, finely
chopped

for the 'pastry'

450g wheat starch
110g potato starch
50ml water

For the filling: defrost and prepare the prawns as appropriate, then mix them with all the seasoning using an electric mixer or by hand. Then thoroughly mix in the winter bamboo shoots.

For the 'pastry': boil the water, add the wheat starch and then the potato starch, and mix thoroughly until they form a doughy texture. Cut off a small amount (2½cm), flatten it using a cleaver, and use circular movements to form a flat circle.

To prepare the dumplings, place a generous teaspoonful of mixture on to the centre of the pastry, and fold it into a half-moon shape. Ruche the edges together, then gently fold back both ends and roll it in the palm of the hand. As the two edges of the triangle become longer, snip them in two with scissors to form ears, and fold them backwards. Repeat for each bunny-shaped dumpling, and steam them in a bamboo basket for about 5 minutes.

Contributors

Simply Heathcotes
Jackson's Row
Deansgate
Manchester M2 5WD
0161 835 3536

Palmiro
197 Upper Chorlton Road
Manchester M16 0BH
0161 860 7330

The Malmaison Brasserie
Piccadilly
Manchester M1 3AQ
0161 278 1000

Le Petit Blanc
55 King Street
off Chapel Walk
Manchester M2 4LQ
0161 832 1000

Lounge 10
10 Tib Lane
Manchester M2 5LN
0161 834 1331

Restaurant Bar & Grill
14 John Dalton Street
Manchester M2 6JR
0161 839 1999

The Lime Tree
8 Lapwing Lane
West Didsbury
Manchester M20 2WS
0161 445 1217

Koreana
Kings House
40a King Street West
Manchester M3 2WY
0161 832 4330

Charles Hallé Restaurant
Bridgewater Hall
Lower Mosley Street
Manchester M2 3WS
0161 950 0000

Juniper
21 The Downs
Altrincham
Manchester WA14 2QD
0161 929 4008

Rhodes & Co
Water's Reach
Trafford Park
Manchester M17 1WS
0161 868 1900

The Lincoln
1 Lincoln Square
Manchester M2 5LN
0161 834 9000

The Lowry
Pier 8
Salford Quays
Manchester M5 2AZ
0161 876 2120

Tampopo
16 Albert Square
Manchester M2 5PF
0161 819 1966

The Yang Sing
34 Princess Street
Manchester M1 4JY
0161 236 2200

Index

Weights, measures and servings

All weights, measures and servings are approximate conversions.

SOLID WEIGHT CONVERSIONS

Metric	Imperial
10g	1/2 oz
20g	3/4 oz
25g	1 oz
40g	11/2 oz
50g	2 oz
60g	21/2 oz
75g	3 oz
110g	4 oz
125g	41/2 oz
150g	5 oz
175g	6 oz
200g	7 oz
225g	8 oz
250g	9 oz
275g	10 oz
350g	12 oz
450g	1 lb
700g	11/2 lb
900g	2 lb
1.35kg	3 lb

STANDARDS SOLID

1 oz	=	25g
1 lb	=	16 oz
1 g	=	0.35 oz
1 kg	=	2.2 lb

LIQUID CONVERSIONS

Metric	Imperial
55ml	2 fl.oz
75ml	3 fl.oz
150ml	5 fl.oz (1/4 pint)
275ml	1/2 pint
425ml	3/4 pint
570ml	1 pint
725ml	11/4 pints
1 litre	13/4 pints
1.2 litre	2 pints
1.5 litre	21/2 pints
2.25 litre	4 pints

STANDARDS LIQUID

1 tsp	=	5ml
1 tbsp	=	15ml
1 fl.oz	=	30ml
1 pint	=	20 fl.oz
1 litre	=	35 fl.oz

OVEN TEMPERATURE CONVERSIONS

°C	Gas	°F
140	1	275
150	2	300
170	3	325
180	4	350
190	5	375
200	6	400
220	7	425
230	8	450
240	9	475